MW01164815

SOUTHERN
ABSOLUTION

by

PAUL FITZ-PATRICK

Wasteland Press

www.wastelandpress.net
Shelbyville, KY USA

Southern Absolution
by Paul Fitz-Patrick

First Printing – April 2018
ISBN: 978-1-68111-229-9
Library of Congress Control Number: 2018938748
Front cover: Absolution Under Fire by Paul Wood, 1891. Collection
of the Snite Museum of Art, accession number 1976.057

Printed in the U.S.A.

0   1   2   3   4   5

ACKNOWLEDGEMENTS

Thank you to everyone who helped me in writing *Southern Absolution*. Since they are all humble in nature, let it suffice to use their first names along with the first letter of their last name. They are: Michael R., Jim M., Jerry C., Kevin K., Jason G., Katie F. and Laura F. "…They did it not out of a sense of history, but out of an act of charity…"

ABOUT THE COVER

A Special thank you to the Snite Museum of Art, University of Notre Dame in South Bend, Indiana, for allowing me to use the cover image. The cover is an image from an oil painting titled: *Absolution Under Fire* by Paul Wood, 1891. Collection of the Snite Museum of Art, accession number 1976-057.

1

Love of Country

This is a story of immigration, similar to others, from the mid-1840s and 1850s. People came to America in search of something better. However, this story is different in the way it played out, particularly for the Sullivan family. It begins in 1845, when the Sullivan family arrived in Waterbury, Connecticut. The Sullivan family had traveled by ship from Ireland, by way of New York City, Bridgeport, Connecticut, and then finally Waterbury, Connecticut.

Joseph the main character of this story, was called Joe by his friends and family. He was the youngest son of Patrick and Ellie Sullivan, and he had two older brothers and a younger sister. The siblings don't play a major part in the story after 1863.

This story begins in 1862, and it was important for Joe because that was the year he went to Jefferson Medical College of Philadelphia. The distance from Waterbury to Philadelphia was roughly 200 miles, but in the early 1860s the trip could take two full days. It took that long for a couple reasons, but the most significant reason was that there was a war going on. Rail service was available but limited for the civilian populace.

Joe's older brothers, who were four and six years older than him, joined the Union Navy early in the conflict. His older brothers were good sailors, and the two had been working on a schooner in New Haven, Connecticut, with the hope of owning their own ship one day. When the conflict began, they both thought the Navy would help them to that end, as well as serving the country they had grown to love.

Joe and his sister Brigid had to help around the homestead when they weren't attending school. Joe's father worked in the local brass factory, but an accident at the factory in 1859 robbed him of the full use of his left leg. Patrick was strong headed with a fighting Irish spirit and forbade Ellie from helping ease the finances.

That changed somewhat when a significant part of the factory workers went to war. Fortunately, Patrick was good with figures and he got a job in the brass factory; first as an accountant and later as shift foreman.

The Naugatuck Brass Factory realized Patrick was more valuable as a shift foreman. He was tough, but fair, and everyone seemed to like him, laborer and boss alike. It was during this time that Patrick finally gave in to his male ego and agreed to let Ellie take a job as a seamstress, with the condition she could work from home.

With Joe's older brothers serving the country, his father thought that was enough of the Sullivan family in service to their new-found land. Instead, he desired for his youngest son to go to college, because that was something he never did and there was currently no draft in place for able-bodied men.

Joe would be the first son of Patrick and Ellie Sullivan to attend college. His two older brothers never had an interest in furthering their formal education.

In July 1862, Joe boarded a train for Philadelphia, where he would attend Jefferson. Joe had an aunt living in Philadelphia, so it was an ideal situation. He would work in his uncle's furniture shop to pay his way through Jefferson.

Joe had a talent for woodwork, especially in delicate details. His talent for woodwork was due in part to the penknife his father gave him when he was twelve. One of the things his father's brass factory produced was penknives. Naugatuck knives were well known, especially in Connecticut. No one could have foreseen that the Federal Army would rely so heavily on the Naugatuck Brass company during the war.

When Joe got the penknife from his father he took to whittling, and he carved nice objects out of wood, providing he could find some. He was always picking up branches and discarded wood; it was almost like a game to him. What he couldn't whittle, his mother would use for fuel to cook and heat the house.

Joe's aunt and uncle in Philadelphia didn't have any grown children, so they appreciated having Joe around the house to help. Wilhelm, Joe's German uncle, was hoping his two young sons could learn something from their cousin from Connecticut. Along with the other things Joe showed his two young cousins, he also taught them how to whittle.

Joe's parents were pleased that Wilhelm and Kathleen could provide a place for Joe to live. They were also happy that his new home wasn't that much different an environment from what Joe was accustomed to. They went to church every Sunday morning, just like they did in Connecticut.

Joe's Aunt Kathleen met Wilhelm when she came over on a steamer, four years before the Sullivans came from Ireland.

Had Wilhelm not been Catholic, it probably wouldn't have worked out. Joe liked his Aunt Kathleen because she reminded him of his mother. She still had a strong Gaelic accent and listening to his aunt and uncle talk could be funny at times. The strong-willed Bavarian, talking with his set-in-her-ways Irish wife, provided some interesting meal conversations. At times, Joe found himself looking toward his aunt at the end of the table, when he couldn't understand his uncle's accent. Aunt Kathleen would translate in a manner of speaking, normally starting out, "What I think your Uncle means…" and go on from there.

Joe's intention was to eventually become a doctor, but he was too young for immediate entry. He took other courses, while attending lectures by physicians at Jefferson.

Joe showed a proclivity for the medical field, probably because of his inquisitive nature of how things worked. When his older brother brought home a badly injured dog, he was fascinated with looking at all the veins, arteries, and muscles that made up a living creature.

He was primarily responsible for keeping the dog alive, and the dog, whom they named Brendan, seemed to know that. For that reason, he was always at Joe's side after his recovery. Brendan died two years prior to Joe's leaving home, and he buried him in their back yard overlooking the Naugatuck River.

Joe was fascinated by some of the lectures at Jefferson, particularly the ones involving surgery. One of the doctors invited Joe for a social at his house, and Joe questioned the doctor about the medical field for most of the evening. The doctor's wife didn't like the constant questions, but the doctor could see something in the young man from Connecticut. He didn't mind it at all, and he even encouraged Joe.

In Philadelphia Joe's schedule was to work at his uncle's furniture store until late morning, and then attend classes and lectures for the rest of the working day. It went on like that until early December, when there was time off for Christmas.

When he went home for Christmas, the Sullivan family got some tragic news. Joe's older brother Patrick Jr., or "Paddy" as he was known by family and friends, was killed in battle. The family took it very hard, but particularly Joe who idolized his older brother. How could he go back to school? How could he not right the wrong done his brother? Those were the thoughts that went through Joe's mind.

Without telling his parents, Joe went to New York City five days after Christmas in 1862 and decided to join the Federal forces. He joined with his cousin, Jack Sullivan and they both volunteered to fight with one of the Irish units. The Irish Brigade had suffered terrible losses at Antietam in September, and again in Fredericksburg,

Virginia, a few weeks before his enlistment. They needed replacements, so the recruitment office was all too willing to sign up a couple of Irishmen from nearby Connecticut.

The talk was that the Union would have to resort to a draft, so Joe and his cousin wanted to get in before that happened.

Joe and his cousin, who had also been through four months of college, were proficient in reading and writing. They were valuable in the sense that they were more literate, and able to understand orders more easily than most of the other soldiers.

In April of 1863, a few months after joining the Federal forces, Joe and his cousin prevented their company from being flanked by the Confederates at Chancellorsville, Virginia. They subsequently received a promotion for acts of bravery.

The majority of what follows is about Joseph Peter Sullivan from Waterbury, Connecticut after Joe's cousin was killed on the 2nd of July 1863, at Gettysburg, Pennsylvania. That is where Joe's story starts.

Absolution is the term given to the effects of the Sacrament of Reconciliation whereby a penitent is reconciled to God and the church community.

While the normal method of the Sacrament of Reconciliation is through what is known as "confession," where a penitent meets individually with a Priest, if this method of receiving the Sacrament is not available due to extraordinary circumstances, the Church allows for the granting of General Absolution.

The most common time when General Absolution is acceptable is during times of "grave necessity," such as during times of war when soldiers are about to enter into battle.

Those surviving the grave situation must then go to the normal form of the Sacrament of Reconciliation and confess those sins that were in their heart at the time the General Absolution was granted.

2

Gettysburg, Pennsylvania

On the 2nd of July 1863, troops from both sides were on the threshold of battle for the second day in a row. Joe was in a position where he could hear Father Corby give final absolution to the Brigade's troops who were about to take part in battle. Here is what Joe wrote regarding that occurrence, in his journal, sometime after the battle, at a place which became known as "The Wheatfield":

> *"Father Corby, who was attached to the Irish Brigade, stood atop a boulder, so the troops could see and hear him. He spoke first about what might happen that day and that some men would meet their heavenly Creator for their final judgment.*
>
> *Father Corby explained that to get the general absolution each man must be sorry in his heart and mind for any wrongdoings. Then he raised his right hand into the air and gave a general absolution and blessing.*
>
> *The prayer for all of us was in Latin, so it was not understandable to all present, but it brought a sense of peace to all who could hear his voice. All the Catholics who could hear him kneeled, and other Christians showed some sign of respect. In fact, I heard from another*

soldier that evening that even General Hancock removed his hat and bowed his head. Then within five or ten minutes of that absolution and blessing, the battle began."

Joe's brigade rushed into battle and the fighting was fierce. After they discharged their muskets, they stopped to reload and both Joe's shots were fired into a sea of gray and brown. He saw two men fall.

It wasn't that he was any better a shot than anyone else, because he just shot into the line of brownish-gray uniforms. It was hard to miss. Maybe the two men he saw fall were felled by someone else's Minié balls. The Rebels kept rushing, however, and he didn't have time to reload. Running forward he speared a confederate soldier and then he was hit by something, and he fell to the ground.

Joe didn't know what hit him, but a powerful force knocked him backwards and his chest hurt a lot. He looked and felt for blood, but there was none. Then he remembered that he put his penknife in his breast pocket before the battle. Joe initially believed a Minié ball hit the penknife, and the force knocked him to the ground.

There was no time to see if that was what happened because it was chaotic. Joe was lying next to a Rebel who was wounded in the left chest area. As he was getting back to his feet, that's when he noticed the Reb was wearing something around his neck. He had never seen one before, but he had heard about it from a Frenchman at his aunt and uncle's parish in Philadelphia.

When Joe got back up, and onto his feet, he was going to spear the wounded enemy soldier, but he couldn't. In the confusion of it all, the wounded soldier looked up at him as Joe was ready to thrust his bayonet into his chest. Time slowed, almost magically, so that everything appeared to happen slower. He saw that the Rebel soldier was grasping his religious medal with his hands as if in prayer.

Something inside Joe told him not to kill the poor soul, so he made sure his bayonet landed to the right of him in the soil. He pulled his musket back out of the earth, and he noticed the soldier's eyes were closed, but his lips were moving. He couldn't hear what he was saying because of all the noise around them, but he was sure he was praying to the Lord.

Instead of killing him for some reason, known but to God, Joe kneeled next to him and tried to attend to his wound. The blood was gushing forth too quickly from his wound and he couldn't stop it. He tried to remember what he learned at Jefferson, but to no avail. He watched as the color rushed out of him and he realized no one could help him. The Confederate soldier did open his eyes, however, and Joe saw his lips move. He thought he was saying, "Thank you for not spearing me. Bless you."

Then the poor soldier's head rolled slightly to his left. He was dead, at least Joe thought so, and he felt bad that a holy man like that died in a field of chaos. He did seem to die a peaceful death, if that's possible, amidst all the killing and noise.

Even though he was dead, he was clutching the medal that hung around his neck. Unmindful as to what was going on around him, Joe released the man's grip from the medal and looked at it. The medal had an image of the Blessed Mother on one side and a big M on the back. Rubbing the blood off, as best he could, there were two small hearts underneath the M.

Then, through the noise of the raging battle, Joe could hear someone say, "Oh no you don't, let him be!"

Joe was brought back to the present by the burly voice and he felt someone pushing him, and it stung. He looked up at who was pushing him with a bayonet, and it was a Johnny Reb with two stripes on his arm. In his daze, he hadn't realized that his company had been flanked by some Rebs. The nearest Federals were about 40 yards away, and the fighting had turned to hand-to-hand, because the Rebs came quicker than they could reload their muskets.

"Let him be," said the soldier, sticking his bayonet into him again, but not piercing him.

"Git up, yir ma prisner," he said in an accent nearly unintelligible to someone who grew up some 700 miles to the north.

Joe got up and looked around. The battle was raging all around them, but he was squarely within the ranks of soldiers from Georgia, as he would find out later. First, he thought he should run back to his lines, but then he had a second thought. What if his captor had a bullet in his chamber? Joe didn't run.

This is what happened next in Joe's own words:

> *"I was brought back to the rear of their lines and I asked the soldier why he didn't shoot me or thrust me through with his bayonet. He replied that he was out of bullets, and he said he didn't spear me because he saw me try to help his fellow Georgian.*
>
> *It was a sweltering day and I was upset that I let myself be captured by a man with no bullet in his musket. We walked about a mile, and I could start to see other soldiers dressed in various shades of gray and brown marching forward to where we had just come from. I considered just running when I had the chance, but the chance never came. That battle raged on until about eight o'clock that night. I only knew that because I heard my captor talking with other soldiers from another company of soldiers.*
>
> *That company had just returned from a battle at the far end of the line and they were repulsed by a unit from Maine. That fight had turned into hand-to-hand fighting, and some of their company were also taken prisoner.*
>
> *They treated me fairly by giving me water. They were going to give me some food, but there wasn't any. There were other soldiers there, prisoners, like myself. However, I was one of only four from our New York unit. We talked amongst ourselves when we were sure we couldn't be heard by our captors. The opportunity for escape never presented itself, but we all knew they would shoot us in our backs if we tried.*

They moved us farther to the rear of their lines late that night, so it had been a long day. It was so hot that the water was hot and unappealing. We walked through a stream, but the swarms of flies and mosquitoes hovering above the water made it a most inhospitable scene.

We could hear our captors talking about how the next day there would be a final push. We could hear shooting all through the night but, due to the heat and noise, it was generally a sleepless night. We were transferred to some other soldiers to watch over us, to make sure we didn't escape.

One soldier, I believe he was from Minnesota, tried to sneak away just as the sun was starting to rise. He didn't make it far, and so as not to waste any bullets, the Rebs stabbed him several times and dragged his body back to where we were grouped. They used his lifeless corpse to make an example of what happens if you try to escape.

The next day, which was 3 July, we couldn't tell what time of day it was, but we could tell the confederates were unleashing an artillery barrage that seemed to go on for hours. The Federals answered the Confederate artillery barrage almost immediately with their own barrage, and you could tell the difference between the two. You could tell because of the distance between the two lines of artillery. When the Federal barrage seemed to stop, the prisoners all supposed that's when the Confederates began their infantry advancement. It was the final push they were talking about the evening before.

Later, we saw some soldiers return and they had sullen expressions on their faces, and some were even crying. We found out that masses of Confederates were cut down in droves, and we heard that one regiment had less than 20 percent of its soldiers remaining at the end of the day.

A fellow prisoner, from Pennsylvania, thought our best chance of escape was that night, while they were licking their wounds. Unfortunately, a Reb soldier overheard the Pennsylvanian and he just walked up and shot him in the chest. There was no warning. He just shot and that was it.

They let his body lay there, as well, as an example of what would happen to anyone else who got any ideas. There was no further conversation that night because no one wanted to risk getting shot. The Rebs seemed more irritable that night, and while we were happy about their fate, no one dared say anything to make them even more ill-tempered.

It was still hot, and we were so thirsty, but our captors didn't treat us as nicely as the night before. We heard that General Lee called for a retreat southward toward Virginia the next day, which was the 4th of July. There was a sense of doom among all the other prisoners, and even some of the Rebels were starting to complain about this and that. Some even thought they could win the next day if General Lee gave them the chance. The Rebs prepared for the Federals to attack, but they never did.

I know I was hoping for the attack, so I would have had the chance to get back amongst the Federal forces. Finally, in the early morning hours of the 4th of July, we started walking toward the south. Though the first night I had been captured had been sleepless, sleep came easy the second night. It was easy because we were exhausted, and it was quiet, except for the occasional screams from the field hospital. It was nice to sleep.

I remember I was having a dream about my two older brothers and we were laughing; then, you could hear a noise like canon fire, and I thought to myself, "Oh no, here we go again," but thank God, it was thunder. The rain began right before the sun came up and it was the first time I could ever remember being happy about rain. Shortly after the rain started someone came and talked to us about what would happen to us.

"You boys will be taken to a prison camp near Richmond and you'll have to walk most of the way, along with the rest of us," the officer told us.

"So, are your forces retreating to Richmond?" asked one of the prisoners, with a smile on his face.

The captain responded politely, "No, but I'm not going to tell you our plans in case one of you tries to escape. Now regarding that, I want to tell you that we expect you all to behave and we'll treat you well. If you try to escape, you'll be shot. It will probably be several days before we get across the Potomac and that's when you'll get your first meal. You might get some biscuits if there are any extra, but don't count on it. Now, you will be asked to pitch in and help at times, and if you don't, you'll get no food."

As the confederate captain continued to talk, I couldn't help but think how similar we were. He spoke very nicely and he would occasionally take off his hat and look up, catching raindrops in his mouth or on his fancy handkerchief which he used to wipe the rain off his brow. One of the reasons I listened so closely was because he resembled my brother, Paddy, who died seven months earlier. I also wondered what became of my other brother, Mark, and whether he was alright.

Joe's daydreaming was interrupted by another prisoner tapping him. Looking at the man who tapped him, the soldier was pointing to the captain, who was looking straight at him. He said, "I don't know where your mind is, but I asked you a question."

"Sorry, sir. My mind was on my brother, and I was wondering how he is. Can you repeat your question?"

"I asked if anyone here has medical training of any type. Do you?"

"Yes, sir. I had about four months of medical school."

"What's your name corporal?" the captain asked.

"Joe Sullivan and I'm from Connecticut."

"Well come with me Joe Sullivan; we're going to put you to work."

Everyone stayed put except for Joe as he followed the captain who was still on his horse. He walked for what seemed like 10 minutes, and Joe saw a lot of wounded soldiers. They finally got to a field hospital, which was probably where he heard the screams coming from during the night. When they got to the tent, the captain dismounted, and he said, "Come with me."

Joe followed the captain into the makeshift hospital, and the scene was not pleasant. They were in the process of cutting off a young boy's right arm and leg. Joe turned as the doctor started sawing and the screams were piercing. He wished he had kept his mouth shut and not mentioned his brief time at medical school. When an attendant took the arm and leg away from the make-shift operating table, the doctor looked up at the captain with raised eyebrows, and said, "What is it, Captain?"

"This is the only prisoner who admitted to any medical training. His name is Joe Sullivan."

"Thanks, Captain. That will be all."

Before leaving, the captain looked Joe in the eyes and said, "If you give the doctor your word that you won't try to escape, there may be a meal in this for you." The captain didn't leave until Joe gave him an answer.

"I give my word to both of you that I won't try to escape."

At that, the captain stuck out his hand to shake and he said, "Well, Joe, I suppose the fighting is over for you now."

Joe watched the captain as he got back up onto his horse and meandered through the mass of soldiers. As he watched, he wondered what job he would be doing. His question was answered shortly afterwards. The surgeon, Dr. Thomas O'Leary, was the captain's brother.

"Well Joe, like my brother said, you are needed here, so don't be a shirker. If you do what I ask of you, you'll do fine and like my brother said, there will be a meal in this for you. Now make sure you drink enough water because I don't want you to get dehydrated. The mind plays tricks on you when you are dehydrated, so prevention is the best rule. You don't need to ask permission, just help yourself," and he pointed to the water container which was a canvas water bucket catching the rain water.

Everyone in the field hospital had worked non-stop for four hours when they got the word that they were going to begin their retreat. They would leave the badly wounded behind. Dr. O'Leary explained that he hoped the Federal doctors would be merciful and do their best for his comrades.

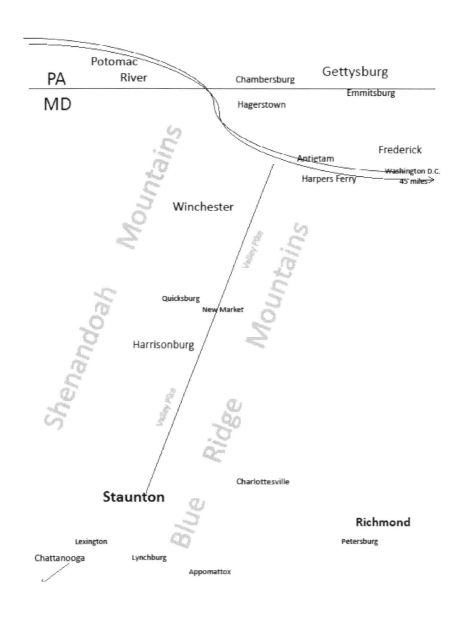

PA

Potomac
River

Gettysburg

Chambersburg

MD

Emmitsburg

Hagerstown

Mountains

Frederick

Antietam

Washington D.C.
45 miles

Harpers Ferry

Winchester

Valley Pike

Mountains

Quicksburg

New Market

Harrisonburg

Shenandoah

Valley Pike

Blue Ridge

Charlottesville

Staunton

Blue

Richmond

Lexington

Petersburg

Chattanooga

Lynchburg

Appomattox

3

Retreat to the South

Joe spent most of his time walking alongside the ambulances and would stop when they stopped. He didn't have a timepiece, so it was difficult to keep track of time, though he didn't know why he worried about time. It could be months before he was set free, so the time of day really didn't matter.

They traveled until it was almost dark, and the rain made the roads slow going. The doctor was as good as his word and he gave Joe some of his supper, which consisted of horse meat and Johnny Cake. Joe came to learn that what the Federals called hardtack, the Confederacy called Johnny Cake, which used corn meal instead of flour. Due to the Union blockade flour was hard to get, so the Confederacy had to use corn meal.

They crossed over the Potomac River and into Virginia on about the ninth day after the battle. Joe's job was to follow the doctor around and help treat wounds, and other horrible reminders of what a Minié ball or cannonball fragment could do to flesh and bone.

The number of ambulances stretched as far as the eye could see, and if it weren't for the rain, the ambulance train could have been overtaken by the Federals. That was fortunate for the confederates but not for Joe. He wondered how long it would take to get to Richmond.

Additionally, there were soldiers hobbling along on make-shift crutches which mostly consisted of muskets or tree branches. The number of walking wounded was equally staggering. They didn't want to be left behind at the mercy of the Federal forces.

At times, the commanders were concerned about the slowness of their movement, so they had to order many soldiers to stay behind. Months later it would come to light that the Confederates weren't pursued by General Meade. However, in the early days of July 1863, the Confederates didn't know that. They assumed the Federals would attack them while their backs were up against the Potomac River. The river was swollen because of the heavy rains, so it was slow crossing. The Federal forces missed an opportunity to make the knockout punch on General Lee's Army.

Joe was surprised they didn't tie him up at night, and that he could actually walk anywhere in the camp. By about the fifth day most of the people knew him by name, and the hardness of their hearts had begun to fade away.

There was a skirmish on the eleventh day as Federal forces were probing to see where the Confederates were headed. Joe could hear the gunfire, but he didn't think anything of it. They brought some of the wounded from that engagement into their temporary field hospital, which consisted of well-worn tents, with wooden planks which had been liberated from barns. The wooden planks served as stretchers and operating tables.

Joe recognized one of the wounded as he looked down on the make-shift table. It was the Confederate captain, the surgeon's brother.

He was bleeding profusely midway down his right arm just above the elbow, so out of instinct Joe grabbed a bandage and pressed as hard as he could on the wide-open wound.

Fortunately, that was the subject of one of the lectures Joe sat through the previous autumn. While Joe couldn't help the wounded

Georgian on the battlefield, he would do his best to help the captain who reminded him of his brother.

The captain's eyes opened and he was looking at Joe, and he tried to speak. Putting his right ear down next to his mouth, the captain asked, "How are you doing Joe Sullivan from Connecticut?"

Before Joe could answer, he heard "How's he doing, Joe?" Doctor O'Leary's excited question came from over his right shoulder.

He turned and looking up at the doctor he said, "Your brother has lost a lot of blood. I applied pressure, but I can't stop it."

"Keep the pressure on it, Joe, but let me see," the doctor said as he stood on the other side of the piece of wood holding his brother.

The captain was unconscious now, and the doctor said, "Joe keep applying pressure, I'm going to try something."

The doctor put his fingers into his brother's wound right underneath where Joe was pressing. He turned away and really couldn't see what the doctor was doing, but now the doctor had both hands in his brothers wound and it looked like he was trying to grab hold of an artery with his fingers. All during this, which was probably the better part of five minutes, the doctor kept his calm. He did stop once, look up and close his eyes, as if he were praying to God.

"I think I got it," he said, "but keep the pressure on it for a while to see if his breathing is alright." After about another ten minutes the doctor said, "Okay, release the pressure."

Joe stepped back and looked at the bloody mess, but thankfully the blood had stopped gushing. Dr. O'Leary looked at him and said, "Joe, you saved his life. I just pray I can save his arm."

Joe went to bed that night and did something he never thought possible. He prayed for his enemy, just like Jesus commanded his disciples. Joe prayed for Samuel O'Leary, his brother Mark, and the countless others engaged in conflict.

The rain started again and fortunately the doctor let Joe sleep next to his brother in the ambulance. He was actually better off than most of the confederate soldiers, who were barely lucky to have a piece of canvas to pull over them. When Captain O'Leary moaned,

Joe reassured him that everything was all right. He also changed the bandage on his wound.

The next morning the captain had a fierce fever and the doctor said he was going to have to amputate his brother's arm. The captain wasn't coherent, and he was talking quite crazy. The look on the doctor's face was one of great concern.

If the surgery was successful, then the captain would be okay physically, but the doctor told Joe how hard amputees generally have it. "My brother will be strong though. He always was and I'm positive he still will be."

The doctor asked Joe to assist him, which he did. Joe had grown accustomed to seeing arms and legs cut off, and he didn't even feel repulsed by it. However, when Captain Samuel O'Leary lost his arm, he wept like he was his own brother.

In that they weren't under attack and were relatively safe, they stayed in place for two whole days. The captain awoke on the morning of the second day and Joe saw him and his brother talking. He noticed that they seemed to be talking about him because they were pointing in his direction. Neither of them signaled for him to approach, so he didn't.

A little later the doctor asked Joe to assist with dressing soldier's wounds, but there weren't any clean dressings. They had to wash the blood out of well over 200 bandages and then put them back on.

Doctor O'Leary said that if, in Joe's opinion, any of the wounds looked worse than the day prior, he was supposed to tell him. Many wounds did look worse, but there was little the doctor could do.

To compound an already tough situation, they were out of nearly everything.

Later that evening when Joe checked on the captain, he asked him to talk with him awhile. Since he was the doctor's brother Joe saw nothing wrong with it. So, he leaned on the tent post by the captain's feet, and he asked him how he felt. After he said that, he thought to himself of how insensitive he was. How would he feel if he had lost an arm?

"It hurts so bad that I want to scream, but I know that won't help the situation, and it certainly won't help the other wounded. So, I say some prayers and try to live with it."

When the captain said he would pray and try to live with it, it reminded Joe of his father. He had heard him say almost those same exact words when he had the factory accident. Joe supposed the captain's injury, however, was very severe and the pain unimaginable. Ether and chloroform were running low, so they had to dilute it, or give soldiers a barely sufficient amount.

"I have heard my father deal with pain in a similar way," Joe answered back. "Does it seem to help?"

"Sometimes it does, but I'm afraid it hasn't helped much with this," as he pointed to his missing right arm.

"Joe, the reason I wanted to talk to you is because I'd like to thank you for what you did for me. My brother says you undoubtedly saved my life. Plus, I'd like to thank you for helping like you have. My brother says you are his best attendant. He says you just pitch right in and don't have to be asked."

They talked for about ten minutes about where Joe was from in Connecticut, and then Joe asked where the captain and his brother were from.

The O'Learys were from near Staunton, Virginia, which he said was still about ten days south. He thought about what he had said, and then he added, "That's ten days if everything is going right."

Captain O'Leary told Joe about his home and how you could see the Blue Ridge Mountains rise up from the valley floor. He reminisced of how he and his brother slept outdoors when they were kids. He also said that those some of his best childhood memories.

Their conversation was interrupted when one of the other amputees cried out, and since none of the other attendants were there, Joe told the captain he would go help.

The other soldier had his left leg amputated that morning because gangrene set in. He didn't help with that amputation, so he was surprised to see who the soldier was. It was the corporal from Georgia, the one who captured him at Gettysburg.

Joe's first instinct was not to help him. However, he could tell the corporal was in significant pain, so he got him a drink of water and put a wet cloth on his head. As he was placing the cloth on his head, his captor opened his eyes, and in the dim light of the tent, he asked, "Aren't you the Yankee I captured at Gettysburg?"

"Yes, I am."

"Well, why is it you're helping me?"

"They needed a prisoner to be an attendant, and so here I am."

Joe learned that the corporal's name was Jedediah, and he was from Savannah. While they were talking, the Georgian reached into his pants pocket with some difficulty. Joe could tell he was trying to get something, so he just watched.

After what seemed like 30 seconds, he pulled out a chain. He extended the chain and said at the same time, "I saw you trying to look at this on Pete. After I took you to our rear I went back to where the fracas was, and I saw Pete's body lying there. He looked so peaceful, and I remembered you were grasping at the chain around his neck."

The Georgian continued with some difficulty, "Figuring he wouldn't need it, I took it off his neck and put it in my pocket. I carried Pete back to our rear later that evening, along with about ten others."

Joe noticed that as Jedediah was talking there were tears in his eyes. Then, Jedediah did something that really caught Joe off guard.

"Joe," he said, "I know now that you weren't trying to steal this off Pete. You were just trying to see what it was." After Jedediah said that, he handed him the medal and said, "Here, you take it. Even though you're the enemy, I feel you should have it."

Taking it from Jedediah's blood soaked right hand, he said, "Thank you. Are you sure?"

Jedediah said in reply, "Pete lived on my street, and he was a great guy. He would help anybody, even when they teased him for being a Catholic. Are you a Catholic, Joe?"

"Yes, I am," he replied.

Trying to sit up, Jedediah said, "Pete would have wanted you to have it then. He was that kind of guy, you know loving your enemies and all." After he said that, he fell back down and grimaced from the pain. Joe changed the cloth on the Georgian's forehead with a fresh one.

There was talk that they would be receiving some laudanum in the morning, and Joe was happy for the wounded soldiers. Fortunately, there was enough whiskey to help dull the pain, or to at least make them think they felt better. As Joe poured out some whiskey for Captain O'Leary, the captain said he was welcome to have some, so Joe did. They talked awhile, and then the captain drifted off. Joe must have fallen asleep about two hours after darkness, and it was the best night's sleep he had had since before the fight at Gettysburg.

What woke him was the noise of a carriage driving up. The carriage had medical supplies and food for the wounded. There were other carriages for the other soldiers, but the doctor said Joe should eat from the medical supply wagon.

Joe looked over at the captain and he had some visitors, so he went to see Jedediah, the only other patient whose name he knew. When he looked down at the Georgian he was very pale. He shook him and his body was hard. Joe signaled for the doctor to come over and the doctor determined that the corporal probably had a clot that went to his brain. He was dead.

Joe and two other attendants carried Jedediah out, so that he could be buried. The burial detail already had several graves dug and they motioned for them to drop the body into one of the graves. After he let go of his body, on impulse Joe put his hands into his pockets as he stood there, looking down into the grave.

He felt something in his pocket and remembered that he had the chain Jedediah gave him the night before. The grave diggers started to throw dirt on Jedediah and Joe told them to hold up.

He jumped down next to Jedediah's body and lifted his head off the dirt. Joe placed the chain with the religious medal around his neck and instinctively made the sign of the cross. When he hopped back up out of the grave, the grave diggers resumed throwing dirt on top of Jedediah's body. Jedediah was covered with earth after a couple minutes, so Joe returned to the field hospital.

Since it was a nice sunny day, the word spread around the hospital that they would be separating from the main force and the wounded would follow. They were on the outskirts of Stephenson, Virginia.

Doctor O'Leary came up to Joe and pulled him aside. He said he wanted to talk with him privately, so they stepped outside the field hospital. Dr. O'Leary looked to make sure no one was listening.

"Joe," he said, "you've been of immeasurable help to me and my brother. We were told that any Yankees we are using to help us are to be turned over to the provost before noon. The prisoners will then be marched south to Richmond, picking up a train at some point along the way."

As the doctor was talking, Joe couldn't help but think about the food. It would become harder to get, if what Dr. O'Leary was saying was true. He saw Joe looking at the ground and he must have known that he was thinking the worst, so he said, "Now I want you to listen closely."

Joe looked back up at Dr. O'Leary's face.

"I've asked for an exception to that order. That exception is for you, if you are interested." He looked in the doctor's eyes with a new-found interest, and the doctor continued, "I asked that you be attached to my brother to watch after him and make sure he makes it home to Staunton. Would that interest you, Joe?"

Joe nodded his head yes and said, "Yes, sir."

Doctor O'Leary continued, "Now I'll tell you the same thing my brother told you when we were leaving Gettysburg. You must promise not to escape and if you should somehow find yourself freed, you must promise not to rejoin the fight. They used to parole prisoners in the beginning of the war, but they found out that the soldiers rarely kept their promise. I suppose I can understand that, no one wants to seem like a coward."

Unknown to the common soldier, neither side was willing to parole any longer, primarily because of President Lincoln's Emancipation Proclamation. It continued for a while afterwards, but in May 1863, paroling was no longer in practice. Besides, if it was still done, Joe would have been low on the list, and probably never be given the chance. A corporal was essentially on the bottom of the list.

When the doctor told Joe that, it sounded too good to be true, especially considering the circumstances.

He looked Doctor O'Leary in the eyes and said, "I promise your brother will make it home safely, and that I will remain in Staunton until the war's end." Joe was going to say until he was freed by the Federals, but he decided not to. There was no reason to get on the doctor's bad side, especially since he was being given an excellent chance.

The doctor looked Joe in the eyes as if he was trying to read his mind, and finally he said, "Okay, I trust you and I trust you'll look after my brother. Now let us go see the provost, and he will give you a letter spelling out what's expected of you."

The provost was a big man and he struck a nerve with Joe. When he handed him the letter he said, "Now take care of this because if you get stopped and you can't produce it, you can be shot as a spy." Joe looked around to see if anyone was smiling and they weren't, so he knew how serious the provost was.

Before the sun reached its apex that hot July day, most of the soldiers took off in a northerly direction. The prisoners kept moving toward the southeast, and the wounded toward the southwest.

The latter group included Corporal Joseph Sullivan. Although he wasn't happy about being a prisoner of war, he preferred that to the fate of the other prisoners who were headed to a prisoner camp near

Richmond. He was sure he would be treated more fairly then the other prisoners.

4

Continuing Southward

They moved out that day at what Joe figured was about three o'clock. Unfortunately, Doctor O'Leary was now attached to the soldiers, so the wounded had no doctors in their train of wounded. That was another selling point to the provost.

Corporal Joseph Sullivan would tend to the wounded soldiers' care. He had overheard Doctor O'Leary making a case for his not being sent to Richmond. He told the provost how Joe could and would help the other wounded as needed.

There was room enough for Joe to sit in the ambulance with Captain O'Leary. The captain wanted to walk like the rest of his men, but his brother made him promise that he would ride in the ambulance for at least a week. Joe sat next to the captain and they talked, but when the ambulance train stopped, he would get out and distribute water to the other wounded.

On one such stop, a wounded soldier fainted from the heat, so he took Joe's space alongside Captain O'Leary in the ambulance. Joe walked alongside the ambulance and kept an ear open in case the captain needed something.

When the sun went down, the wagons stopped and Joe helped set-up tents and an eating area. They relied on the generosity of the people of the valley, as Captain O'Leary referred to their present geographic location. While they didn't seem to have much, the people brought what they could, mostly corn meal and green apples.

That night, Joe figured they probably completed only five miles, but it was five miles closer to Staunton, as the captain said. There was no place set-up for Joe to sleep that night, so he tossed one of the mule blankets on the ground underneath the wagon. The captain decided he wanted to sleep outside, too, so Joe got another blanket for him.

"What did you do before the war, Joe?" the captain asked.

"I was in my first year of medical school in Philadelphia."

"You couldn't get a deferment?"

"I suppose I could have if I tried, but I got word over Christmas that my older brother died in the war."

It was difficult for Joe to speak about his brother Paddy and that's why he never had, even though Captain O'Leary reminded him of his eldest brother. The captain continued with his questioning.

"I'm sorry, Joe. Our country has paid dearly with the blood of fathers, sons, brothers and cousins. Is that why you joined?"

"Yes. Paddy was in the navy, but I didn't like going on boats as much as my brothers did. Therefore, I went to New York, so that my parents didn't know what I was planning to do. I joined up along with my cousin, Jack."

Joe was uncomfortable talking about his brother, so he wanted to change the subject. "Captain, if I may ask, do you have any other brothers or sisters, besides the doctor."

"Yes, Joe. We have two older sisters who are both married and living near Richmond. One brother-in-law is in the Navy and the other is a doctor, like Thomas. However, I don't know where either of them are at present. News has been sparse."

The captain got sleepier as they talked and finally at a lull in the conversation he dozed off. Joe wasn't quite as lucky as the captain though, and he laid there for what seemed like hours. He wondered about his brother Mark, and where he was and what kind of boat he was on. As he lay there, Joe wondered how his mother was doing and whether she had been notified about him. He was sad for her, because she had already given up one son for the country, and she didn't know about his fate. Did she think he was dead? He hoped not.

Joe wondered if his mother has seen his cousin's mother at church, and how she was dealing with Jack's death.

It was difficult seeing his cousin cut down by musket fire, and he couldn't get the image of the blood gushing out of Jack's head. He thought back to the battlefield, and how he was knocked down, and wondered why that was. Why couldn't it have been his cousin Jack? It must all be part of God's plan, he thought.

Finally, Joe fell asleep. He slept soundly until he felt someone shaking him and saying his name, so he turned over and noticed that the captain's wound had somehow opened. The captain was applying pressure to the bandages.

"Let me see that," Joe said, and he reached to look under the blood-soaked cloth.

"Do you think you can stop it, Joe?" The captain asked.

Before answering the captain, Joe looked at his stump and the blood seeped from the stitches. Joe put pressure on the stump and told the captain to lie back down. Kneeling beside the captain's right side, he said, "I don't know if I can. It's too bad your brother is gone because he would certainly be able to stop the blood flow. I don't understand how it started bleeding again."

There weren't any doctors in their long train of wounded, just the three attendants, and one of them was the Yank from Vermont. Like Joe, he also had a letter from the provost and was helping out. Even if he wanted to help the captain, the Vermonter's knowledge of medicine was less than his own.

"Captain, I don't think you should travel because it surely won't stop bleeding if you keep moving your arm."

"What do you suggest, Joe?"

Looking out over the landscape, which was still green from the rains four or five days prior, Joe saw a church steeple. Maybe there was someone at the church who could help him, so he said, "I can see a church steeple up ahead, and maybe we can find some help there."

The captain nodded his head and he decided that he and Joe would visit the town and catch up with the wagons when they could. Captain O'Leary spoke to the other captain, whose dialect Joe could hardly understand. Captain O'Leary and the other captain, whose last name was Linden, worked it out. Captain Linden had a less severe wound, but he couldn't fight.

Captain Linden said they would continue following the valley to the south. Captain O'Leary and Joe, on the other hand, would stop in the town by the name of Winchester.

The stop in Winchester was a nice respite from the southern push towards Staunton. Joe was near Winchester in the Spring, but with the Federal forces. He couldn't walk through the town now as he could in May. It was a pretty place, and the apple trees were full of green apples. The captain did all the talking and they found a doctor who could help him.

The doctor was old, so he liked hearing that the captain's brother was a doctor in the Army of Northern Virginia. He looked at the amputation and decided it wasn't that bad, he just added more stitches. The doctor didn't have any laudanum for the pain, so the captain endured with great fortitude.

While the doctor was stitching the captain, he kept looking at Joe very curiously. Since Joe didn't utter a word at the recommendation of the captain, the doctor asked him straight out. "And how about you young fella, where are you from?"

Joe didn't answer. He looked over at the captain, and the captain nodded to him, so Joe said, "I'm from Connecticut, doctor." Before the doctor could ask another question, Joe said, "I'm the captain's prisoner, and I gave him my word I wouldn't try to escape."

Captain O'Leary explained to the doctor that paroling soldiers was no longer used or encouraged. However, they thought it would be less of a drain on the Confederate army to use a prisoner than to use a fellow Virginian, who would be more beneficial to the army.

They stayed in Winchester three days and were treated very well. The people of Winchester were as bad off on food supplies as the rest of the Shenandoah Valley, but at least they gave the captain and Joe some fatback and hominy. The fatback could be made into a nice stew along with the hominy and some cut up green apples.

The Applegates, an older couple, offered to put the captain up, but they didn't want a Yankee staying on their property. The captain was insistent that if he couldn't stay, then neither would he. The Applegates relented and the two stayed with them, and it worked out well. Joe had to do most, if not all the chores.

Listening to the captain and the older man talk reminded Joe of when his parents had visitors drop by. Instead of talk about the factory, however, Captain O'Leary and the Applegates talked about farming. There was little talk of the war and for good reason. The older couple lost two of their sons at Antietam, so Joe could understand their feelings toward him.

They had one more son, who they were happy to have out of harm's way. He was too young to join up, but he was adamant that he would join when he turned 15, which was just the week before. The captain asked where their son was, and they seemed to think he was near Harrisonburg.

When the captain shared with the Applegates what happened in Gettysburg, they were brought to tears. Mrs. Applegate said something very insightful, "Wars aren't what you think they are. The men can't wait to fight, thinking it will be over quickly, but the days turn to weeks and the weeks turn to years and there's still fighting. It takes a terrible toll, but mostly, on the mothers of the lost boys. God help us all, south and north alike."

The Applegates were just warming up to Joe when they left for Staunton. The parting was tearful, in some ways because Mrs. Applegate gave Joe a hug and whispered in his ear, "Joe, I'm glad for your mother's sake that you got captured and are looking after Captain O'Leary. You seem like a good boy. May God bless you and protect you both."

5

The Valley Pike

From Winchester they headed south, with Joe pulling the captain in a cart hitched to a mule. They didn't make good time, and at times it was dreadfully hot. They decided not to take the Valley Pike, which as Joe learned from the captain, traced its roots back to before the Europeans colonized the Americas. Staunton was about 100 miles away, and as Joe would soon discover, it sat at the base of some mountains.

The captain explained that before the English came to Virginia, a host of native tribes used the route as a migratory hunting path from Georgia all the way to Canada to hunt. The only two native names Captain O'Leary could remember were the Delaware and Catawba tribes, and Joe said he wasn't familiar with the latter tribe.

Captain O'Leary felt they shouldn't take the Pike because it had been well foraged. The captain said they would be more likely to find food off the well-traveled path. There was a less traveled road at the base of the mountains, and that's what they used.

Joe would learn from the captain one night that the Valley Pike played a key role in General Stonewall Jackson's Valley Campaign the summer before. The captain's brigade was part of that crucial campaign.

The going was slow, and the mule was of very little use. Joe could walk faster than the mule, but he couldn't pull the makeshift cart. At least the captain could lie down in the cart, as small as it was. Due to the extreme heat, they took frequent breaks which slowed them down. Joe after all, wasn't in any hurry. He would rather be with the captain then with the prisoners who were headed to Richmond.

It was offensively hot, but occasionally it would rain and cool the temperature down. The one benefit of that was the sunset was spectacular.

Both Joe and the captain enjoyed the evenings the most. They would hear gunfire at times, and Captain O'Leary thought it was just someone getting supper. They hadn't eaten in the three days since they left the Applegates, but then their fortune changed.

The captain saw a rabbit and shot it with his pistol. He asked Joe if he ever cleaned a rabbit, and when he was slow to answer he said, "You go get it, and I'll clean it as best I can, with your help. Then gather some wood for a fire, and we'll have some rabbit for supper."

Joe was never so hungry, and the rabbit tasted good. Some coffee would have been a real treat, but they were lucky to have water, which was the result of a late afternoon thunderstorm. The water was cool and did not taste bad like the water in their shared canteen.

"Joe, can I ask you something personal?" The captain asked.

"Yes sir."

"Please Joe, call me Sam when no one is listening."

"You've had more than one opportunity to escape. Why haven't you?"

Thinking about the captain's question, Joe looked him plainly in the eye, and spoke. "Well, in a way, I owe you since you saved my life, and I gave you my word."

"I understand the latter, but what do you mean, I saved your life?"

"Sam, it's sort of hard to say, but I guess it stems from what Mrs. Applegate said. I was luckier than her two oldest boys. I've been thinking about when you all took me prisoner, and how odd that was."

"What was odd about it?" Sam asked.

Joe explained the events near the battlefield and how he was knocked to the ground. He told Sam how he was surprised by being knocked to the ground, and how he had felt for wounds. He couldn't find any, so he got up. Then, when he was going to spear the soldier who, he may have shot, there was a look in his eyes. It was like his eyes spoke to him.

Joe explained how the soldier was wearing something around his neck, and when he kneeled beside the soldier, the soldier thanked him for not spearing him. As he was looking at the medal, he was captured. Then, Joe explained how the next day, when he saw all the soldiers walking back, he felt sorry for them even though they were the enemy.

"Do you believe God was watching out for you?" Sam asked.

Grinning at Sam, he said, "I've played that over and over in my mind, and that's the only way I can explain it."

"Joe, you're a good man. I wish I could pardon you once we get to Staunton, but we're not allowed to do that anymore. You understand that, don't you?"

"Yes. I know. Like Mrs. Applegate said, I'm lucky to be alive. I hope their youngest son is okay. Will we be going through Harrisonburg?" Joe asked.

"Yes, we will."

And while Sam didn't ask, he thought he knew what Joe was thinking. He wondered to which unit the young Applegate boy was attached. That was a thought he tucked into the back of his mind, or at least until they got close to Harrisonburg, which he figured was still over a week away. A week that is, if there were no surprises and the mule held out. The mule was very slow, and they couldn't make it go any faster.

There were thunderstorms nearly every afternoon for a week. While the fresh water was nice, it made travel slow going. The mule eventually took its last step, and it couldn't go on. Since they couldn't get the mule to go on, the captain put it out of its misery.

As Sam cut into the breast of the beast, which he thought was the best part of the mule, a foul odor made him cover his nose. As hungry as they were, Sam decided they might regret eating the poor beast. Perhaps that's why it was unable to go on, because it was sick and diseased.

For the next two days, Sam tried walking. His bravado got the better of him, though. Perhaps if it were cooler it would have been a different story. They were pretty much left alone when they did come across anyone, which surprised Joe. That was probably because the blue tint of Joe's uniform had been drowned out by the dust, the mud, and the blood. It wasn't Joe's blood; it was the blood from all the Confederate soldiers he tended to, including Sam's.

When the two approached other people, Sam would do the talking, for good reason. When Joe spoke, it was very apparent he wasn't from Old Dominion or for that matter any state below the Mason-Dixon Line.

Finally, after two days of walking, without the mule, Sam could not walk any longer. Joe helped him along, but they needed a break from the day-in and day-out drudgery. They stopped south of Quicksburg.

The name of the town was a contradiction as to their progress. In fact, there was nothing quick about their progress. Joe would come to find out that it was there that Sam fought in the Battle of New Market.

As the two sat on a kind farmer's front porch, Sam simply stated, "There was quite a fight near here. Both sides lost many fine soldiers, but your side took a real beating." They sat quietly pondering this as time passed by.

After two days there, and some nourishment, Sam felt fit for travel. He tried to talk several of the local farmers out of a horse or a mule, but they were desperate themselves for lack of nearly everything. Joe and Sam started out mid-morning and walked a good distance. Sam figured they could make it to Harrisonburg in a day if the weather held. They did make satisfactory progress, but not to Harrisonburg.

Along the way to Harrisonburg, they stopped to fish. Joe was fortunate to catch a fish from a nearby stream within minutes of putting the line in the water. The line was from Sam's jacket, more precisely from the officer's braid from the bottom of his right sleeve. While his brother buried his arm after he amputated it, he thought Sam might want to hold on to his officers' braid. Ever so carefully, Joe unwound the braid and got it out of the jacket. Joe used one of the safety pins that held up what was left of Sam's sleeve for the hook.

Joe didn't know what kind of fish it was, and Sam thought it was a trout. Sam admitted that he didn't care for fish, but they had their most nutritious meal in two days.

As they were sitting around the small fire, Sam asked Joe a question. "You liked the Applegates didn't you, Joe?"

"Yes, I thought they were fine people, especially Mrs. Applegate. She gave me a hug before I left and said something about a mother always loving her children."

"Why do you ask?"

"Well, I've been thinking about their young son in Harrisonburg, if that's where he still is. It sure would be nice if I could rescue him, so that Mrs. Applegate isn't left sonless."

"Yeah. What do you have in mind, Sam?"

"I don't know, but I still have about a half a day to figure it out. However, I will need your help and cooperation. I may have to say some unkind things about you, just so you know."

"If it helps the Applegate boy, I won't mind, and I'll even play along."

Joe had also been thinking about the Applegate boy, and he was ahead of Sam in the planning phase. Of course, Joe didn't know the layout of Harrisonburg, but army camps were army camps.

The two sat around the dying fire and finished the last of the fish.

They hatched a plan for the next day, assuming Sam could talk their way into the camp. Both Joe and Sam heard some animal sniffing, but the animal must have realized that the two men cleaned the fish to the bone. It was relatively quiet, except for the sniffing, and the sound of an occasional fly buzzing around. Both drifted off to sleep around an hour after dark.

The two were so eager to get going in the morning that they didn't even think about their stomachs. As they got closer to the army camp, after about three hours of walking, the sun was high in the sky, and they could smell the camp fires. There was something about a wood fire that always makes one feel like eating. That fact, wanting to eat that is, was all the keener when they passed through the outer pickets. Like in Winchester and Quicksburg, Sam did all the talking.

Sam asked to see the adjutant, and when the sentry asked who was asking, Sam stood strait up and looked the soldier in the eyes. "Captain O'Leary is asking, private." By the tone of the way Sam said, "private," the private realized he was being a bit cavalier in his manner. Perhaps the young man couldn't see Sam's rank, or that most of his right arm was missing.

Sam's change of tone got the private's attention, and he said he would go tell the adjutant that he wanted to see him. Looking around the camp, Joe was struck by how similar the scene was to one of his Federal camps. He couldn't recollect where, but it was a scene that probably played out in just about every camp, both North and South.

There were people sitting around, there were people playing cards, and there were people singing and strumming on makeshift guitars. Then, of course, there were soldiers cleaning guns and waiting in line to use the blacksmith's stone to sharpen blades.

"The adjutant will see you now, captain. Right this way, please."

Captain Willis Longley was younger than Sam by perhaps two years. He was tall and like Sam, he suffered the consequences of war. Captain Longley may have been taller, but it was difficult to tell since his left leg was a peg, and he waddled when he walked. It was the first artificial leg either of them had seen, but it wouldn't be the last.

Putting out his left hand, Sam said, "Captain Longley, I'm Captain Samuel O'Leary, and I have a favor or favors to ask of you.

Corporal Sullivan and I haven't had a decent meal in well over a week, and I was wondering if we could share a meal."

"Yes, Captain. You may be our guests."

"I'm curious though, why is this Yankee with you?"

Joe thought it was hard to tell that his uniform was blue, but Captain Longley apparently had a keen eye.

Sam thought a minute about the question and told him the story of Joe's being captured at Gettysburg. In that Joe had some medical experience, he was placed in the ambulance detail. He told him that he did a very good job, and that he helped save more than one of the South's sons. Then he explained how his brother, who was a surgeon, tasked Corporal Sullivan to stay with and help him after his arm was amputated.

Looking for a clue as to how the story was being received, Sam continued by telling Captain Longley that once Corporal Sullivan got him to Staunton, he would be turned over to the local provost for transport to a prisoner of war camp. He went on to say that he was growing weaker by the day, and he couldn't keep up his guard. He said that while he thought Joe was an honorable man by the way he had helped him thus far, he believed it was only a matter of time before he would jump at the chance to escape.

Captain Longley nodded his head while Sam was speaking, and Joe couldn't help but notice him looking at him with an untrusting eye. "Captain O'Leary, what is it you are asking of me?"

"I wonder if you could detach a soldier to accompany me and this Yankee corporal to Staunton. I don't believe we will see further fighting until autumn. I would be beholden to you."

The captain took in what Sam told him, and then he looked outside his tent at Joe. He cleared his throat, and said, "I believe we can spare a recruit."

"Yes, about that captain. I have a specific recruit in mind, if he is assigned here. You see, I stayed with a family when I was in Winchester, the Applegate family, and as a small way to make amends to them, I'd appreciate it if you could assign their son to me to help me get to Staunton."

"That's highly irregular, Captain O'Leary. If he's here I'm not inclined to detach him to you, since you seem to know about the boy. It's understandable that you need help to get to Staunton, but the choice should be left up to me."

Sam took a chair and sat down opposite Captain Longley. He didn't say anything at first, but just rubbed his right arm where it was just a stub. Captain Longley didn't say anything either, waiting for Sam to respond, which he did.

"You know, Willis this war has gone on longer than we all thought. I don't know about you, but I was sure it would be over by the first Christmas. I gave my arm for Virginia, and you gave your leg. In a way, that's a small token of our allegiance because the Applegates gave two sons. They were killed at Antietam. I'm not saying their third son won't meet that same fate, but if I can change the odds, I'd like to try."

Sam's speech was from his heart, and he struck a nerve with Captain Longley. He reached for a stack of papers that looked like a roster. He then asked, "Captain, do you know the Applegate boy's first name?"

"I believe it is Caleb."

Looking through the roster he found a Caleb Applegate. "It looks like he's brand new. He came in a few weeks ago, right after the unfortunate occurrence at Gettysburg. Let me send for him."

"Thank you, Captain Longley," Sam said.

While they were waiting for Caleb Applegate to appear, Captain Longley sent another private to get some food. At first, he asked the private to get food for just Captain O'Leary, but when Sam raised his eyebrows and glanced at Joe, he corrected himself. "Get enough food for the prisoner, too." At that, Sam smiled an approving glance toward the captain.

The private who went for the food came back with some Johnny Cakes, boiled peanuts, and two cups of coffee. They were both pleased to get the provisions, but especially the coffee because it had been at least a month since either Sam or Joe had any.

When Caleb Applegate showed up to the provost's tent he thought he was in trouble, as evidenced by the look of concern on his face. The look of fear turned into a smile, however, when Sam told him that his parents gave them lodging about two weeks ago.

Caleb knew his brothers were dead, but it was still hard for Sam to talk about Caleb's brothers in the past tense. Sam wished he remembered Caleb's brothers' names but he couldn't. It would have been more personal to use their names instead of the impersonal, "your brothers."

Captain Longley stayed and listened to the conversation while Captain O'Leary told the boy why he was summoned. After he explained everything, Caleb looked towards Captain Longley and asked, "What happens after I see the captain to his home?"

"I'll give you a letter, addressed to the garrison commander in Staunton, and tell him you can be attached there. Do you understand, Private Applegate?"

"Yes, sir. Should I go get my belongings?" he asked.

"No, Captain O'Leary will be staying the night, so he can see our doctor. Report here after morning reveille."

And at that, young Caleb Applegate saluted and went about his business. There was a bounce in his step as he left the tent. Joe searched his mind for anything to relate to. None came to mind, but then he remembered something from back in April when they were near Chancellorsville. The company adjutant had summoned him, and he thought he was in trouble.

When he got to the adjutant's tent he remembered how relieved he was that the adjutant only had a question regarding Connecticut. Joe could answer the adjutant's question, which simply involved the name of a river near New London.

Though Joe had never been to New London, he did remember the name of the river because it had the same name of the one that flowed through London, England. It was the Thames, and Joe learned that from his parish priest. Joe also remembered that his older brothers had occasionally sailed from New London.

Even though he was in the enemy's camp, Joe felt good. The respite from the walking was welcome, not to mention the food. It wasn't as good as the food he would have had with his regiment wherever they were. However, he realized he was a lot better off than the prisoners taken to Richmond. Joe calculated in his mind that they should have gotten there the week before. He wondered if they were fed along the way, and he tried to remember some of the names of the other prisoners.

There was no stockade for Joe, so they assigned a sentry to watch him. He missed Sam's company, but there was nothing he could do except endure the night under watch. He was, after all, more fortunate than countless others.

They played the same reveille as in the Union camps, so when it blew, Joe thought he was dreaming. When he tried to get up and go about his business, the sentry pointed his musket at him and said, "Where do you think you're going, blue boy?"

Joe stopped in his tracks, collected his thoughts, and said, "The latrine, if it's alright with you."

The sentry didn't reply right away because he was sore that the blue boy, as he called him, had a good night's sleep and he hadn't. "Well, all right, but be quick about it."

Sam almost talked himself into getting a horse, but the supply sergeant said it was needed to move supplies towards Richmond. Without a horse, it would take them at least three days to get to Staunton. A healthy person could make it in one or two days, but Sam was greatly affected by the heat. Caleb Applegate showed up about halfway through breakfast; when Sam found out that the young lad hadn't eaten, he told him to go get some food before they left.

Joe had gotten accustomed to talking with Sam on a first name basis, but realized he better call him, sir or captain, while they were in the company of others. It was already warm by the time they started walking south towards Staunton and, unfortunately, the day would only get hotter.

Spoiled by a day of rest and two meals, Captain O'Leary requested that they take a slower pace. There was little to no conversation all day, and Caleb didn't know what to make of the Yankee who was accompanying them. Caleb was cautious, but polite.

6

On to Staunton

Since their route paralleled a stream, Sam took frequent breaks. At every stop, he would do the same thing. He pulled what looked like a woman's garment from beneath his jacket, dunked it in the water, and put it over his head. Joe wished he had a piece of cloth or something to dunk, but he didn't. He entertained the idea of cutting off a portion of his pant legs.

Since there was no reprieve from the heat the next day, Joe did cut off both pant legs, about mid-calf. When Joe took out his penknife to cut off the bottoms of his pant legs, Caleb had a concerned look on his face. Though he didn't say anything to Joe about it, he walked over to Sam, and asked him something which was inaudible. Joe noticed Sam smile, and heard him say out loud, "I don't think that will be a problem, private. He's had that knife ever since he was captured at Gettysburg. He's had plenty of opportunities to use it on me, but he hasn't."

In a way, it was good that Caleb asked Sam that question because there hadn't been much talking up to that point. It was difficult knowing what Caleb was thinking, and that led to more questions.

"So, how were my folks?" Caleb asked.

Sam and Joe looked at each other, and Sam spoke. "They were well, but they were concerned for you. I was surprised by how your parents, especially your mother, handled your two brothers' deaths."

Before Sam could continue, Caleb said, "Yeah, my mama is a religious woman, and she has great faith in God. My daddy has more difficulty than my mama. Of course, he tries to keep up outward appearances."

That night the three sat and talked, and it was really the first time Caleb saw Joe as just another soldier like himself. That may have been because Sam told Caleb what his mother said to Joe. Caleb looked at Joe, and Joe said, "Your mother is worried about you, so make sure you stay safe and don't do anything foolish once we get to Staunton."

For the next two days, the heat was unbearable. It was the same both days. It got terribly hot, followed by a late afternoon or evening thunderstorm. After the rain, the air was so thick you could cut it. Caleb caught a rabbit, but when he skinned it their joy turned to frustration when he said it wasn't fit to eat. Joe didn't know how Caleb knew that, but he was too embarrassed to ask.

Caleb disposed of the rabbit about 30 feet from where they were sleeping, and they could hear something in the night feasting on the carcass.

They talked the next day about what happens when an animal eats bad meat. No one knew the answer for sure, but it provided something else to talk about, other than the distance they traveled and how far they had to go.

That night, Joe and Caleb found out what the cloth was that Sam would wet whenever they got to a stream. It belonged to Sam's wife, whose name was Sara Ann. Sam finally shared some aspects of his life before the war and Sara Ann, in particular. Sam married her in 1858, more than two years before the war. She was pregnant with child the last time he saw her, and he was worried about how she would react when she saw him. Sam also mentioned that he was upset that he wouldn't be able to play very well with his son, at least nothing that would require two arms.

Joe thought about what would happen when they got to Staunton the next day. He thought about his promise to Sam's brother, but he couldn't help thinking about escaping. Thinking about his promise, Joe rationalized in his mind that if he saw Sam to within a day of Staunton, then he essentially kept his promise. However, he was unfamiliar with the territory, had no map, and he was literally surrounded. The fact of the matter was that he would stick out like an orange in an apple basket even if he did manage to escape.

Joe wondered what Sam was thinking regarding his situation. Would he put in a good word for him? Or, would he not give it a second thought due to the war? These thoughts went through Joe's mind, and he started to pray. He prayed that his guardian angel would protect him, whatever his fate. He prayed that the people of Staunton would treat him fairly, and not blame the whole war on Joe Sullivan, from Connecticut. Joe didn't just pray about his plight. He prayed that Sam's wife would accept her husband's circumstance with mercy and love. Joe also prayed that Caleb wouldn't get caught up in the fighting, and that if he did, that he would be safe.

When they reached Verona, Joe had a perfect opportunity to escape. In fact, Sam encouraged him to leave while Caleb was trying to catch a fish in the nearby creek. Sam told Joe he would probably be safe if he used the mountain ridges, as he headed north.

"No, but I sure do appreciate your gesture. I promised your brother."

"Darn you, Joe," Sam said. "Be realistic, if you leave now I won't have to turn you over and you might have a chance of getting far enough north to run into your army. I can't guarantee your safety if they take you to Richmond. It's getting crowded there, and I fear for your wellbeing."

Joe smiled while Sam was talking, and he knew in his heart that he would be alright. He wasn't being as calm deep down as Sam said or imagined. He was afraid of being on his own in a land where people would string him up from a tree if they had the chance. No, he believed he was doing the right thing by staying with Sam, so he put his trust in God.

Caleb was successful. He caught three fish, and he had them cooking over a fire in no time. Discussion over dinner was about Jesus. Since Caleb joined them, it was the first time the subject of religion came up, and it was Caleb who mentioned it. Specifically, how Jesus prepared a meal for his disciples after His resurrection.

All three were familiar with the story, and they each talked about it in a similar way. It was Joe, however, who said that that simple act by Jesus, showed how He loved his disciples, and Jesus meant what He said about being a servant to others.

Early the next morning they were awakened by a hideous noise. It was two or more animals fighting, but they weren't sure what they were fighting about. It was difficult getting back to sleep after that, so they started walking at first light.

They got to Staunton before noon, and Sam was anxious to see his wife and son. They walked quite a way before reaching the city proper, and a passerby in a wagon noticed Sam, and stopped up ahead. The old man got down off the wagon, and said, "Sam, your brother sent word you were coming. Everyone was worried about you." Sam stopped cold in his tracks, and said, "Daddy, is that you?"

Sam told Joe later that he didn't recognize his father at first, since he was much skinnier then when he last saw him.

Father and son hugged. Sam didn't require two arms for that. Sam's father had to wipe tears from his eyes. He stood back, looked at his son and asked, "Does it hurt, son?"

"Occasionally, but I am lucky to be alive."

Mr. O'Leary looked at the two-people accompanying his son, and asked, "And who are these two? Your brother sent word that you were being escorted by a Yankee prisoner."

"Sir, the one there in the cut off pants is Corporal Joseph Sullivan, from Connecticut, and the other young lad is Caleb

Applegate, from Winchester. He was detached to accompany us from Harrisonburg."

Mr. O'Leary stepped towards Caleb, put out his hand, and said, "I appreciate your helping my son." He didn't mention anything or even look at Joe. While Joe expected that, Sam was hurt that his father treated Joe so uncivilly.

"Father," Sam said, "Joe here saved my life on more than one occasion, and I'd appreciate a little courtesy his way."

After Sam said that, he realized he had never spoken to his father in such a tone. However, his father didn't seem fazed by his son's tone and stepped towards Joe and put out his hand and said, "Son, please excuse my behavior. I'm mighty beholden to you."

Mr. O'Leary helped his son up into the wagon, and Caleb and Joe followed suit. It wasn't far to Sam's house, and Joe just laid back and enjoyed the fact that he wasn't walking.

Caleb listened to Mr. O'Leary and the captain talking, and he wondered if he would ever have the chance to talk to his father again. Tears came to his eyes as he thought about his two older brothers, Joshua and Isaac, who were killed the year before in Antietam. The date was engrained in his mind – September 17th.

Caleb and his parents took their deaths hard, because the war should have been over by then. At least that is what everyone believed. When they got the news of his brothers' deaths, they tried to make it sound like their deaths spared the Confederacy a defeat. Joshua and Isaac were with Major General A.P. Hill's Division, whose troops rushed in from Harpers Ferry to Antietam to avert a route by the Federals.

The Confederate left flank was being overwhelmed and Hill's Division plugged the gap and stopped that from happening. The fact that his brothers helped avert a defeat, was of little comfort to his mother who grieved the deaths of her two eldest sons.

Caleb didn't feel any animosity toward Joe, even though he was from the enemy. He'd spent four days with him, and he could have been one of his own brothers because of the way they got along. He admired Joe for keeping his word that he would get Captain O'Leary home and not try to escape. Truth be told, if he had tried to escape, Caleb wouldn't have minded.

That morning when Caleb asked Sam what he should do when they got to Staunton, Sam said he should accompany them to his homestead. Then he could eat some home cooking, spend a restful night, bathe and then he would give him a letter of explanation to the Staunton garrison commander. Caleb asked what would happen to the prisoner, and Sam just said that he wouldn't have to worry about that, that he and his father would handle it. As for Sam's reunion with his wife, Sam's concerns were for naught.

When they road up to Sam's house, Sam's mother was holding the baby while Sara Ann was hanging laundry on a clothesline. She recognized the noise of her fathers-in-law's wagon, but she kept hanging the clothes while talking with Sam's mother. When she did look up at the wagon she dropped the shirt, she was about to hang, and ran to Sam. Sam didn't have difficulty holding his wife, mother and the new addition to the family. His son was behind the house and when he heard his grandmother calling for him, he came running. Joe was happy for Sam, and he stood there smiling at the joyful reunion.

Caleb left the next morning, and Sam's wife and mother gave him a similar sendoff to the one Sam and Joe got from the Applegate's when they left Winchester. Whereas the Applegates had little food to spare, Sam's mother gave Caleb some cornbread and a pie to take along. In parting, Sam held Caleb with his good arm and said, "Boy, don't do anything foolish that will make your mother and father childless. Please, feel free to come to visit if you have some free time. We'd enjoy your company."

Caleb even came to Joe and said, "Well, Yankee, I hope to see you around."

As it turned out Caleb would be attached to a unit guarding the rail yard right there in Staunton. Unbeknownst to Joe, Staunton was important to the Confederate war effort just by its geographic

location. It was a crossing point between the Shenandoah Valley and
Richmond. Also, unknown to everyone at that parting, Staunton
would be important the following June.

Caleb would live until the end of the century and beyond, and
he would make his parents, grandparents seven-times over. What no
one knew, besides God the Almighty, was that Caleb and Joe's lives
would cross paths years later in Northern Virginia.

Though food was scarce in the valley, there was plenty for Sam's
homecoming, and the O'Leary family included Joe in everything.
There was no talk of what would happen to Joe, so he was always
wary when Sam had visitors.

One night, about a week after they arrived in Staunton, two
soldiers rode up. Joe was splitting wood, so he could see them talking
to Sara Ann on the front porch. Joe had a sinking feeling in the pit of
his stomach, and rightly so. After all, here Joe was in the heart of the
Confederacy, with an axe in his hand, and no one to watch him.

Joe continued to split wood, and he would occasionally see the
soldiers looking his way. Once when Joe was looking towards the
porch, he saw Sam motion to him. It looked like Sam wanted him to
come to the house.

As Joe walked towards the house every possible situation went
through his mind. He could run, and possibly make it to the nearby
river, and hope for the best. Or, he could see what was in store for
him. Since Joe trusted Sam, he walked the 100 or so yards to the
porch to see what his fate would be.

"Corporal," Sam said, "These gentlemen were sent to pick you
up and deliver you to the stockade."

Joe didn't say anything, he just listened and assumed one of the
two soldiers would speak next, which they did.

"Corporal, as a Yankee prisoner you should be put somewhere
for safe keeping, besides here. The captain, however, has suggested an
alternative. You can lend his farm a hand," and when the soldier said
that, he was embarrassed for not being more careful with his words.

Realizing the soldier's dilemma, Sam said, "Corporal Sullivan, what the sergeant is trying to say is that you will help out at the farm here. Our farm is crucial to the war effort and, as such, you will work your way into the good graces of the Confederacy. Since I lost an arm to your brother Yankees, you will replace that arm by working here. You need to give your verbal word that you won't try to escape or wreak havoc on the local area."

Joe looked at Sam, and then turning towards the two soldiers he said, "I swear that I will help here on the farm, and will not cause a commotion, or wreak havoc, as the captain said."

Sam smiled at Joe, and turning to the two soldiers, he asked, "Will that do, gentlemen?"

The soldier who hadn't spoken yet asked if the captain would give them a letter to their commander, as well as a written statement from Corporal Sullivan. Sam indicated that wouldn't be a problem and he called for his wife to bring two sheets of paper and two pencils. In that Sam couldn't write, he asked Sara Ann to write what he spoke. While Sam dictated the letter to Sara Ann, Joe wrote what he had just said to the soldiers.

When the soldiers rode off, Joe breathed a sigh of relief. Turning toward Sam, he said, "I won't let either of you down, so help me God."

"I know you won't Joe, you've proved that countless times. Now, let's get some supper."

Joe worked as hard as any three men for the next two weeks, and when Sam commended him on his work, Joe asked a favor. He asked if he could ride into town with them on Sunday and go to the Catholic Church, if there was one.

Sam thought about Joe's request, and said, "There is a Catholic Church, but I don't know how often they meet. I will ask around, though. I believe they have a new priest because the previous one had to leave."

And while Sam didn't elaborate on why the priest, a Father Downey, had to step down, Joe would find out over the course of the next several months what happened. Apparently, the priest shot someone, and he went to trial several times. When the case was finally solved, it was ruled self-defense because the priest was trying to protect his housekeeper. Even though the priest was cleared, his bishop wouldn't let him continue to serve because he didn't think it was right that a priest would use a gun on a man.

The priest, who was sent to replace Father Downey, was an Italian Jesuit named Father Joseph Bixio. He was well liked, and it was from Joe's contact with Father Bixio, that he would see his own life take a different direction. Every Sunday for the next nine months or so, the O'Leary's would drop Joe off in front of St. Francis of Assisi Catholic Church, and he would wait for them to pick him up again later that afternoon.

Joe liked Father Bixio, and the feeling was mutual. Father Bixio loved hearing about Joe's childhood in Connecticut. Father Bixio had a habit of stopping Joe mid-sentence and saying, "Could you say that again?" He particularly loved Joe's stories about what his parents would do at Christmas. The Italian priest would sit back in his chair and close his eyes as Joe told him the Sullivans Christmas story over and over.

When Father Bixio inquired about the family's lineage, Joe shared with him how he and his family moved to America in 1845. Both the Sullivans and the Gearys, Joe's mother's family, were from County Wexford in Ireland. They were more fortunate than the tens of thousands who were affected by the potato famine. Fortunately, Aunt Kathleen, who had lived in Philadelphia for a year-and-a-half, had written and said what a great country America was. The Sullivan family was fortunate because they left Ireland with more than the shirts on their backs.

Joe's oldest brother, Paddy was eight, Mark was six, and Joe was two when the Sullivan family made that voyage. Joe was too young to remember the conditions of the voyage like his two brothers and his parents. He explained how his mother was pregnant with his sister when they made the ocean voyage, so Brigid was the only one of the Sullivans born in America.

Joe could only tell Father Bixio what his parents told him of how they got to Waterbury once they got to New York City. He could, however, remember their childhood church, St. Peter's, and how it was too small for the growing Irish Catholic community, so they built a new one to replace St. Peter's. Joe shared some of his fond memories of the dedication of the new church in 1857, which was given the name Immaculate Conception. Father Bixio smiled when Joe told him that. To go with his smile, Father Bixio said, "How fitting."

When Father asked Joe about his parish priest, Joe recounted fond memories of Father O'Neil and Father Hendricken. He remembered that Father O'Neil was very committed to everyone and would work alongside parishioners at the factory, so he could hear their troubles and perhaps provide some instant consolation by way of a prayer.

It was Father Hendricken, however, who Joe really admired. He told Father Bixio enough about his two parish priests that he said, "It sounds like your parents, along with your priests, did you well."

While Joe couldn't understand how such nice, God-loving people, could feel the way they did about slavery or secession from the Union, he didn't want to give Sam cause to get upset at him. Therefore, he never brought up slavery or even states' rights.

The closest Joe ever came to doing that was once when he was riding with Sam back from dropping off some produce. Sam didn't answer directly but, he paused, and said, "I often wonder about that." Joe realized by the troubled look on Sam's face and the tone of his voice, that those two subjects were difficult for him to talk about. He never brought them up again, but from what Joe could see, very few, if any people owned slaves in the area.

As to the reason for the war, he remembered something Mrs. Applegate said to the effect that war is never like you think it will be.

It won't be quick like the politicians tell you and it drags on and on, and you lose your loved ones and your livelihood.

About a month after Joe was settled in at the O'Learys he asked Sam if he could write a letter to his parents to let them know he was alive and doing well. Sam said he would consider it, but his gut instinct was that they should leave well-enough alone. Sam didn't want to call unnecessary inquiry into their arrangement, that is, that Joe was remanded to Sam until war's end.

A real turning point happened on about the seventh Sunday, when Joe spent the afternoon with Father Bixio after Mass. Father asked him a question.

"Joe, will you accompany me to the military hospital in town? I realize that I will have to clear it with Captain O'Leary first," he said. "If it is okay with you, I'll ask him when he picks you up."

Father Bixio did ask Sam if he could take Joe to the hospital, and he explained why. The why was because Father had heard of Joe's brief period in medical school, and he thought Joe could take the place of one of the attendants one day a week. When Father Bixio asked Sam that, he remembered back to when Joe saved his life. Sam knew that Joe could make a difference in other soldiers' lives, just like he did for him.

Sam and Father Bixio got along very well; so, with Sam's approval, Joe accompanied Father Bixio to the military hospital six days later. It was on a Saturday. Most of the soldiers they visited had amputated limbs. Since he had witnessed a lot of that following the battle at Gettysburg, it wasn't a difficult sight for Joe.

Father Bixio wanted Joe to see what he thought were three of the more serious wounds. Joe prepared himself for the worst, but when they walked into the room where the three were, there were just three men sitting and staring at the wall. There were no apparent wounds, and when Joe turned to Father Bixio for an explanation, Father said, "These, I'm afraid, are the worst wounds."

The priest went on to explain that the three men were suffering in their minds, and they only seemed to get worse as the days drew on. He explained that the men who lost limbs knew what their crosses were. However, these three men suffered repeatedly the trauma of what they saw or did.

"You see that tall one there," Father said as he pointed to the one on the end, "Well, they say he was the only one left in his company. They discovered him two days after the battle under a pile of his friends."

Then Father asked, "Joe, in your medical training, did you ever have any experience in things of the mind?"

Joe hadn't, but he said he had heard about such things.

"You know, Joe, I believe these men will have it the hardest after the war. They have no apparent physical wounds, so they will be subject to ridicule. I don't know that the war will ever be over for these poor souls."

During that first visit to the hospital, Joe met a nurse named Angela Quinlan.

Joe remembered Angela all week and couldn't wait until his next visit with Father Bixio. Father Bixio could tell that Joe was attracted to Angela, so on about the third visit he excused himself and left the two alone. They weren't really alone because the three soldiers were there, but they talked freely.

Father took the opportunity to visit with the other soldiers while Joe and Angela talked. He was gone about a half hour.

Angela asked Joe about the north, and Joe tried to find out all he could about Angela. What struck Joe about Angela was how beautifully simple she was. Simple in the way she dressed, the way she spoke, and even in the way she laughed. He particularly liked the way she laughed. Joe noticed one time when Angela was laughing that one of the soldiers smiled and nodded his head. She had been talking about some of the pranks her older sisters played on her as a child.

Joe mentioned the smiling incident to Father Bixio, and he said, "That's terrific! I will tell one of the doctors and see if he will let us try something different."

"What do you have in mind, Father?"

"Heal them with love, my boy. Heal them with love."

Each Saturday for the next eight weeks, Father Bixio, Joe, and Angela would spend time with those three men. They would talk about funny things that happened when they were children, and then turn to the men and ask them by name if they had any such memories to share. The three men's names were: Robert, Martin, and John. It was on the ninth Saturday that there was great progress.

When Angela asked the three if any of them had anything to share, John and Robert raised their hands. As Father and Joe looked at each other in amazement, Martin also raised his hand.

One by one, starting with Robert, they all shared something precious from their past. All three spoke slowly and deliberately, and at times would wipe tears from their eyes. While that was astounding, what was even more special was that when Father and Joe stood up to leave, the three said that maybe they could talk more next week. Father thought about that for a moment and said to the three, "would you all like to come to my church tomorrow? Maybe we can have a picnic afterwards."

"Can we?" The three asked almost as if they were one.

"I can make that happen. Angela and Joe will pick you up, and then bring you to church and back. I have one favor to ask of you though: I'd like you to shave and bathe, and maybe put on some other clothes that Joe will bring for you tomorrow. Does that sound like something you could do for me?"

All three men nodded their heads and smiled. It was almost as if the weight of the world had been lifted off their shoulders.

When Angela said her goodbye to Father and Joe, she said, "I'll make sure they are ready tomorrow morning. If you can get here by 10:00 then I can make sure they change into the clothes you bring them, and that way we can make it to Mass by 11:00."

Father Bixio never shared with Joe that Angela was Catholic, not that it would have made a difference. He liked her, but since she knew he was a prisoner he didn't think he had a chance for her affections.

On the ride back to the O'Learys Joe asked Father why he thought the men made such a dramatic recovery. Father said his prayers were answered, and he explained that he started a novena after their first visit. This was the ninth Saturday, so his novena was complete.

When Joe sat at the dinner table that evening, he shared the day's good news. Sara Ann was in another room, tending to the youngest child, when Joe told Sam about the miraculous occurrence. They could hear her say, "praise God," from the other room, and she came out holding the young one while trying to get a night shirt over his head.

After Sara Ann left the room, Sam told Joe how nice it was of him to help Father Bixio and especially, the soldiers. Sam had seen the effects of battle on some men. Some were strong willed, but then something would make them draw into their shell, like a turtle. His brother had also seen several cases, but he never could figure it out. They both concluded that physical wounds you can heal, but mental wounds were harder to cure.

Then Joe told the O'Learys about Sunday and asked if he could leave for church about an hour-and-a-half before usual, and then he explained why. When Joe told them the part about Father asking the men to shave and bathe, Sam asked where Father would get his hands on three sets of clothes. Joe didn't know, but he explained how Father Bixio seemed to have a knack for procuring things.

Sara Ann told Joe that she would clean his clothes for the special occasion, to which Sam said he thought it was time to give Joe a pair of clothes that they were saving for him for a special occasion.

The next day the O'Learys took Joe to the church to pick up the clothes that Father had promised the soldiers and then they took Joe over to the hospital. Joe could have walked. However, because of the arrangement they had with the authorities, he should be under Captain O'Leary's watchful eye.

Angela was waiting out front when the wagon pulled up, so Joe wanted to introduce her to the O'Leary's. She looked beautiful in a Sunday go-to-church dress, instead of her dingy, blood-stained nurse's uniform. Joe brought the clothes inside while Angela talked to the O'Learys. She remembered a Doctor O'Leary from before the war, and she wanted to ask Sam and Sara Ann if they knew how he was doing.

The three soldiers were happy to leave the confines of the hospital. They sat in the next to last pew, and they sat very still during the Mass. Joe had described what would happen during the Mass, and he said they could do what everyone else was doing, or they could just sit. The three men chose the latter, but they soaked up everything that was said and done.

After Mass, they all sat outside in the back of the church with the sun streaming down on them. Somehow, Father Bixio assembled a meal of fried chicken, fried apples, and even an apple pie for dessert.

For conversation, they all went around the group of six with them saying what they were thankful for. Father Bixio started.

Joe learned a lot from that experience and he tucked it away into his memories of that day. Each of the soldiers said basically the same thing. They were thankful for Father Bixio, Angela and Joe, and they were also very thankful for the nice picnic.

Sam picked Joe up about an hour before the sun went down, and on the ride back to the farm, Joe shared what happened at the picnic. He specifically mentioned how the soldier by the name of Robert included in his thanks a hope that the war would be over soon and everyone could return home.

7
A Time of Thanksgiving

The O'Learys had something to be thankful for during the autumn harvest, because Sam's brother, Doctor Thomas O'Leary, had three days leave to spend at the O'Leary homestead. He was on his way to what was believed to be the next engagement with Federal forces. Joe was happy to see the doctor, who asked Joe to call him Thomas, like the rest of the family.

Sara Ann was the one who mentioned to Thomas that Joe helped at the hospital every Saturday. She even told him about the success with the three soldiers who were not of sound mind.

Thomas found that interesting and asked Joe for the details. There were really no details that Joe could remember, but he told him about how Father Bixio said they would heal the men with love and prayer. Joe told Thomas about the picnic a week prior, and how marvelous it was to see the happiness on the men's faces.

When Joe and Thomas were alone later that evening, Thomas told Joe how thankful he was that he had honored his promise to get his brother home. Joe didn't say anything. Thomas went on to say he also appreciated his helping his brother and sister-in-law, to which Joe did answer.

"You know Thomas, in a way, I'm indebted to your brother. If it weren't for him, I would be in a camp for prisoners, and I highly doubt they eat as well as I've been eating. They certainly aren't treated as well as I've been treated. Besides, your brother is a good man, and he reminds me of my older brother who was killed last November near Norfolk. So, while I can't share good times with my brother anymore, I can share these times with Sam, like he is one of my brothers."

Thomas didn't say anything, but Joe could tell he was thinking.

"You know, Joe, I'm glad you are here as well. From what I have heard, conditions are not desirable at the camps in Richmond and they will only get worse as the war continues. They had to open a prisoner camp in Georgia, and I hear the conditions there are dreadful and will only get worse, too."

Thomas took a sip of his coffee, he was obviously saddened by what was happening. He tried to smile, but he had an anguished look on his face as he continued.

"I fear the war won't be over any time soon. The word out of Washington, from what we understand, is that the Federals will keep the pressure on and try to wear us down by attrition. They seem to have better leadership now, and they realize that Virginia is the key. I fear we won't be able to adjust our strength from one end of the state to the other because they will hit us in all directions."

After reflecting on this a minute, Thomas switched the conversation from war back to things more personal.

"You know at supper, it was nice to see my brother laugh, and I could tell that was a relief to Sara Ann, too. I believe he has his confidence back, and I have no doubt that you have something to do with that. Thankfully, you are doing more good here than you know. What are your plans after the war, Joe? Are you going back to school?"

Before Joe could answer, Sara Ann brought her oldest son in to give Uncle Thomas a kiss goodnight. After he kissed Thomas, he ran to give Joe a kiss, too.

Joe had unexpectedly become a part of the O'Leary family that night, by the simple kiss of a child. He blushed when the child ran back to his mother's arms.

The pause gave Joe time to think about an answer to Thomas' question, but he couldn't think of anything. He just mentioned that he dreamed about going back to Connecticut, and maybe living on the beach for a while. His brothers had a place on the beach, so they could be close to the sea. God willing, he will help Mark with his boat if he gets one after the war. Plus, he wants to spend some time with his parents and younger sister. While Joe was thankful to be with the O'Learys instead of a prison camp, it still wasn't home. Though he didn't mention that to Thomas, he understood, and said, "Well, I hope for all our sakes, that will be sooner than later."

The next morning Joe accompanied Thomas to the hospital. Angela just happened to be in view from the entrance and, when Thomas saw her, he said, "Look at that, could that be the young Quinlan girl?"

Joe answered Thomas, and he said that it was.

"Hasn't she grown into a beautiful woman?" Thomas said, with a smile on his face.

Joe never mentioned Angela to Thomas and figured he shouldn't. After all, he had told Thomas the night before that it was his plan to return to Connecticut at war's end. He rationalized that even if Angela was interested in him, he believed it wouldn't be fair to ask her to go north with him.

When the two climbed down from the carriage Angela saw them, and she ran to the two men. She recognized Dr. O'Leary, but she had something to tell Joe. She just smiled in Thomas' direction, as she made her way up to Joe.

"I'm so glad you came today, Joe. Robert and the others asked to see you at the earliest opportunity. Looking at Thomas, she said, "How are you Dr. O'Leary?"

"Hello Miss Quinlan. It is a pleasure to meet you after so many years. How is your family?"

"They are as well as can be expected under the circumstances. My daddy says he is thankful they had all girls. He feels bad for the other mothers and fathers who are grieving the loss of a child."

Joe excused himself and asked if he could go see Robert and the others. That would give Angela and Thomas time to catch up on all that had happened since they last saw each other, three years prior. Joe thought about Thomas' comment when they rode up, and the way he looked at her and kissed her hand when she presented it to him. Joe realized that he shouldn't be a barrier between the two, and he would stay in the background while Thomas was visiting.

When Joe walked into the room where Robert and the others were, he noticed they were all working on something. It looked like they were building a model of some kind. When Robert saw Joe, he got up and walked over to Joe and shook his hand.

Joe said, "Angela said you all wanted to see me."

"Yes," he said, "I would like to ask for your forgiveness for killing so many of your boys in blue."

"I don't understand," Joe said.

"Father Bixio said that part of our problem was that we need to ask forgiveness of those we've wronged, and you are the only Yankee we know. So, we would like to ask for your forgiveness."

John and Martin put down what they were working on, stood up and joined Robert. They similarly shook Joe's hand, and each one asked Joe's forgiveness.

Joe was speechless, but then he found the words, "I forgive you all. And I'd like to ask forgiveness for any of your brothers I may have killed or wounded."

Shortly after that, Angela and Thomas came to see how the four were doing. When they walked into the room, there was an air of happiness because the three soldiers and Joe were smiling and laughing. Angela introduced Doctor O'Leary to the soldiers and each one shook his hand, and said, "We're so happy to meet you, doctor. Could we have a word in private?" Robert asked.

Joe and Angela left Thomas with the soldiers and went outside. As they walked along the corridor she brushed up against him by accident, as she was trying to step over some clothes that were on the floor. Joe reached down and scooped the clothes up, so no one else would trip over them, and Angela was horrified. She said, "Joe drop those right away! They may be infected."

He dropped the clothes, and Angela told him that they were there because they cut them off a dead soldier. They weren't sure why he died, because he had no visible wounds, so they put his clothing there until they could burn them.

Joe accompanied Angela on her rounds, and he was glad he did. The way she interacted with the soldiers seemed to make them feel good just by her presence. He knew that he liked being around her, and he was glad Thomas asked him to go along. Joe was happy that he got to see Angela two times that week.

On their way back to the O'Leary farm, Thomas asked Joe why the three soldiers wanted to see him, if he wasn't being too nosey. Joe told him the reason, and Dr. O'Leary was amazed that they would do such a thing.

He asked Joe why he thought they did that, and he recounted what Father Bixio told the soldiers. Part of the key to unlocking the hurt in their minds is to deal with it directly. Joe tried to explain as best he could about reconciliation, but he stumbled. Thomas asked, "Are those soldiers Catholic?"

"No, they're not."

As they rode the rest of the way, not a word was said, but Thomas was thinking. He was thinking that he could possibly help other men that were struggling with things locked in the recesses of their minds.

As they got closer to the farm they could make out a dispatch rider, dismounted and talking with Sam. They could tell Sam was reading something, and when they got up to the picket fence, the dispatch rider climbed back on his horse and rode past Thomas and Joe. Thomas had a feeling the dispatch was for him, and he was right.

The dispatch read that he was to leave immediately and rejoin the division. When Thomas asked Sam where he was supposed to report, Sam handed the paper to him.

"Well, brother, duty calls. What a shame, I was looking forward to Sara Ann's apple pie. If I leave in an hour, I can make it half way there before dark."

Sam found it difficult to put on a happy face, and in fact, he said, "That doesn't seem fair. They told you three days, Thomas."

"I know, brother, but at least I was fortunate to get to visit a while. Who knows, maybe this will be over by Christmas." Thomas knew in his mind that this terrible conflict showed no signs of ending, and he feared the tide had changed against the Confederacy. He knew the Confederacy was just delaying the inevitable.

They couldn't produce materials like the Yankees could. Thomas recalled that Joe said his father worked in a brass factory; he wondered if the factory produced anything for the war effort.

On a more personal note, Thomas was upset that he couldn't treat his soldiers properly, and that he had to remove so many limbs to prevent gangrene. If he had time, he thought he could have saved many a limb by trying to get circulation back. But, there was scant time in the war, and he feared things would only get worse.

Thomas dared not voice his opinion out loud, because many dreamed of a Confederate States of America. He was pretty sure his family felt the same way he did, but he had to be a rock for them all.

As Thomas mounted his horse, with all his belongings attached, he rode off towards the northeast. He wished he could have stayed, but "duty calls," he told himself. Still, he would have liked to stay another day or two. He liked that morning, and especially seeing Miss Quinlan. She was pretty and kind. He wondered if she would still be there when he returned after the war.

He realized he was older than Miss Quinlan by ten years or more, but that wasn't unusual. He knew of men who married women half their age. Still he wondered if there could be a chance for them after the war.

Thomas even imagined himself returning to Staunton after the war and starting a medical practice. He also imagined Angela at his side as his nurse. Daydreaming about the future made the ride more pleasant, and the miles flew by. He also wondered about what Joe would do after the war. Joe said he wanted to lay low for a while and spend time with his family in Connecticut. Thomas was impressed with Joe and hoped that he would continue his medical schooling.

Thomas thought about the evening before. While Sara Ann and Sam were attending to the children, Joe had asked Thomas to come out to the barn with him. Joe was very secretive, but he wanted his opinion on something. They climbed up the ladder, and to the left Joe had something hidden in the hay. He pulled out an old blanket, and there was an arm wrapped in it.

Joe had come across a felled poplar tree and when he picked it up he couldn't believe how light it was. He brought most of the tree into the barn, sawed off what he thought would be the perfect length, and he whittled it into what looked like a man's right arm. It was beautifully sculpted, and it even had fingernails. At least they gave the appearance of fingernails.

Joe wanted Thomas' opinion. He wondered if Sam would see it as an insult. He told Dr. O'Leary it wasn't quite finished yet because he wanted to stain it and put some leather straps on it, so that it could be attached to his stump. The top of the fake wooden arm had a place to insert the stump, so that it was attached to the shoulder with a leather harness worn around the neck. It wouldn't be for everyday use, but for special occasions, Joe added.

Thomas didn't think Joe would insult his brother, and he even found himself starting to tear. "He will not be insulted, Joe. He will be touched that you are worried about him. Does Sara Ann know?"

"No, that's why I was hoping you could ask her. Unfortunately, you have to leave."

"Like I said, Joe, Sam will be honored that you think so highly of him, and that you know the trials he has had to go through."

Thomas thought back to how artificial limbs, as they call them, were just coming into being. The Confederacy would only issue artificial legs, because that would at least allow a man to plow a field. Artificial arms aren't quite as functional. Thomas wondered if there would ever be a functioning artificial arm.

As he rode, he thought about how Joe Sullivan had become part of the family. Joe, in fact, said Sam reminded him of his brother Paddy who was killed the previous November in the blockade of Norfolk. He remembered how Joe's eyes teared the night before whenever he talked about his older brother.

It was much the same way his eyes watered when he thought of how Sam nearly died. His prayers were answered that night; the night he had to remove his brother's arm.

As the daylight ran out, Thomas found a place where he could rest for the night. If all went right, he would report the next afternoon to where his dispatch directed him. As Thomas was getting ready to retire for the evening, he pulled out the food Sara Ann packed. As he ate the chicken legs, he thought about how tired he was of cutting off arms and legs, and he wished the war would end. He hoped for the day when people died from old age and not war.

8

Good News in Connecticut

The next day, in Waterbury, the Sullivan family had reason to celebrate. Ellie thought her youngest son was dead, so when she opened the letter she let out a little scream. It was a scream of joy, if there could be such a thing. Patrick wasn't home yet, so she had to save her joy until he got home from the factory. She would have to prepare a special dinner, preferably one that her Joe liked.

The letter, which was smuggled through picket lines of both sides, recounted young Joseph's whereabouts, and lastly it said that he was as well as could be expected in such a conflict. It said he was a prisoner in Staunton, Virginia, and he was better off than all the other Federal soldiers taken prisoner at Gettysburg. Whoever wrote the letter said that Joe wanted to contact them, but that his guard didn't think it would be wise. To authenticate the letter, and to show it wasn't a fancy tale, the writer said, "Joe longs for sitting near the Christmas tree with his mother, father, and his sister, Brigid, sipping on some fine Irish whiskey. He also thinks of Mark at sea, and hopes he is well. Lastly, Joe wants you to know that he is able to receive the sacraments regularly." The letter was signed "J.B."

Ellie wasn't sure if she should let anyone in the army know, so she would wait until Patrick got home from work and discuss it with him. In the meantime, she went and got the Christmas decanter and put it on the mantle. She would wait till Patrick asked why the Christmas decanter was out, before she sprung the good news on him, unless of course she blurted it out before her husband asked.

In that she couldn't share the good news with anyone, she did the next best thing which was to go say a prayer at church and light candles by the statue of Mary. Ellie knew that the Blessed Mother would protect her children both living and dead. She was just so thankful that Joe was alive and not dead as previously thought.

There were several women in Immaculate Conception when Ellie walked in, and among them was Mary McGivney whose husband was Patrick's boss. She wasn't going to tell any of the women the good news until Patrick knew. She lit a candle, prayed for Paddy, Mark and Joe; and then, after leaving the church, she returned home.

She could hardly wait for her husband to get home, so she busied herself with dinner. Unfortunately, Ellie couldn't prepare one of Joe's favorite dishes because they were out of most everything. Dinner would have to be some chicken broth, one potato split three ways, and some bread. It wasn't fancy, but Joe would understand.

After Patrick arrived home from work, Ellie gave him time to get washed and sit next to the fire to warm himself. His leg bothered him in the cold and the warmth of the fire seemed to help. As Patrick was warming his hands over the fire he saw the decanter, and he looked towards Ellie. "Tis four weeks till Christmas, my dear, why is the decanter there?" as he pointed to the bottle on the mantle. She smiled at her husband and walked towards the fireplace. When Patrick said, "Well?" she handed him the letter.

Patrick looked at the letter and it had some funny markings on it, but nothing to indicate the postal service. He opened it and started reading the short letter which was neatly written. The date, October 1863, was written in the top right-hand corner. As he read the letter his eyes welled with tears. He looked up at the decanter and then at Ellie and said, "This is splendid news and I am just so happy, but let's not pull the cork. Let's wait till Christmas Eve, in honor of Joe and Mark. Perhaps they will both be home by then."

The two were nearly delirious with joy, and when Brigid came home just before dinner, they all experienced that same joy over again when they told her the news. Not knowing whether they should let someone in Joe's regiment know about the letter, they decided it was probably best to keep it to themselves. If J.B. had been so cautious, and Joe's guard didn't think it wise to write, they would also let it be. They all went to bed that night more joyful than they had in previous five months knowing that Joe was out of harm's way.

The son who was lost was found again, and they read that particular verse from Luke's Gospel after supper.

9

Prodigal Son

With Thomas gone, the mood of the O'Leary's house was sad. Joe went about his chores, but there was less to do with a fresh cover of snow on the ground. Regardless, he spent a lot of time outside in the barn working on Sam's arm.

Joe decided that Sam and Sara Ann needed time to get over Thomas' departure, and having him around might have stirred up some hard feelings. While Joe felt at home, and thankful for his arrangement, it still didn't feel like his home. That afternoon Father Bixio paid a visit to the O'Learys.

The real reason for Father Bixio's visit dealt more with Joe than the O'Learys. He explained that the hospital was dangerously low on medicines and supplies and he wanted to ask Joe something. What Father Bixio had in mind was that he was going to see if he could procure some much-needed medical supplies from the Federal forces. He told Joe he wanted to run his idea past him before he asked Sam, to see if Joe would be willing to go along with him.

What Father Bixio proposed was to take Joe along in case they crossed over Union lines. Father Bixio said that he could vouch for his identity as a Catholic priest, if the need ever came. Joe said he would go along as Father Bixio wished, but that the final decision was up to Sam. The Italian priest already knew that, but he wanted to get a sense for how Joe felt about it.

Initially Sam protested because of the agreement he had made with the military commander. That arrangement was that Joe was supposed to be under Captain O'Leary's watchful eye. However, when Father Bixio explained the seriousness of the medical situation, Sam gave in. Part of Sam's reluctance was that if Joe was caught, he could be hung as a spy.

Father Bixio and Sam finally agreed that Joe could accompany · him, and they would leave the next day. The next day was Sunday, and Father would celebrate Mass at St. Francis, followed by another Mass in Harrisonburg later in the day. From Harrisonburg, Father Bixio and Joe would head north searching for some Federal forces and some much-needed medical supplies.

Dinner that evening was special. Sara Ann put up a nice ham, the one she saved for Thomas, but couldn't serve due to his early departure. She served sweet potatoes and carrots with the ham. After dinner, Sam and Joe sat around the fire while Sara Ann put the children to bed.

As they sat watching the embers, Sam got choked up on his words, when he was talking about what Father Bixio and Joe had in store. "You know Joe, if you get repatriated by the Federal forces, you will put me in somewhat of a pickle." Joe thought about what Sam said, got up, put another log on the fire and sat back down, but closer to Sam, so he could talk in a quieter voice.

"Yeah, I thought about that Sam. And, if you ask me not to go I won't. I understand how fortunate I've been since Gettysburg and realize that if I was sent to a prisoner camp, well, who knows what would have happened. You've been like my big brother, and I can promise you that I won't outwardly seek to be repatriated. Father Bixio and I talked about that, and I gave him my word that I wouldn't. I'm more worried about your soldiers and their medical needs. However, it is like you said, I could be hung. I don't think God would let that happen though. I believe he saved me at

Gettysburg, and I believe that between the Almighty God and Father Bixio, I will be alright."

Sam thought some sipping whiskey might be nice, since it could be the last time the two were together to enjoy such a comfort. When the last of the embers faded, Joe went to pack a few warm clothes for his travels before he retired to bed.

The next morning Joe gave Sam the arm he had been working on. If he did get caught or repatriated he did not want the arm to be hidden in a pile of hay in the barn.

When Joe handed him the arm, Sam's eyes grew very wide, and his smile was as wide as his eyes. He thanked Joe, and said he was glad he never confiscated his whittling knife. Sara Ann was so overcome with joy that she wrapped a big piece of salted ham so that Joe and Father Bixio could eat well on their journey.

After handshakes and hugs were exchanged, Sam took Joe to Saint Francis for Mass and to meet up with Father Bixio. Sam did something he never did before, he stayed for Mass.

Father Bixio's sermon was comforting, and it just so happened to be about the prodigal son. He wondered if Father Bixio did that on Sam's account, or if that was what his sermon was supposed to be all along. Regardless, it was comforting because everything worked out for everyone, except for the fatted calf.

Mass in Harrisonburg was much like Mass that morning, and Father's sermon was tailored to a smaller audience. When Mass was done, they were invited to the postmaster's house for supper. The postmaster, Edward Sullivan, was pleased that there would be another Sullivan in the household that night. He tried to retrace his lineage, to see if they came from the same county in Ireland; they didn't.

What Joe didn't know was that Father Bixio had filled the postmaster in on what they were going to do. However, there was another parishioner at supper, so Father Bixio didn't want to ruin their plan before they even had a chance to put it into action. That other parishioner, as it turns out, would affect the outcome of one of Father Bixio's future expeditions.

After breakfast the next morning, they left Harrisonburg in Father's wagon pulled by his two borrowed mules. The postmaster's wife gave the two travelers enough food for the day, but if they ate sparingly it could be enough for two days. Whenever they came upon Confederate troops, Joe was supposed to play like he was mute, and it helped. They made it through several picket lines.

After three days of slow riding north from Harrisonburg, they came across a Union cavalry regiment, who didn't even stop. They must not have seen them as an immediate threat. The closest town was Front Royal.

Joe remembered passing through the area with Sam on their way south, but now they were on the well-traveled Valley Pike. Joe preferred the greens of the summer than the browns of late autumn. All the leaves had fallen from the deciduous trees, so the only green was in the pines.

On the fourth morning Father Bixio disappeared into the covered wagon and changed, while Joe took the reins. They had just passed through a Confederate picket line. What Father Bixio didn't share with Joe was what he was going to do, so when the priest emerged from the back of the wagon in a Federal soldier's uniform, he was surprised.

Father Bixio explained that he procured a Federal soldier's uniform from a wounded soldier he visited in a Federal camp the spring before. Joe learned that Father Bixio visited the camp on his way back to Staunton from Chancellorsville. Father Bixio thought the uniform could come in handy one day; this was the day.

Father Bixio had learned from the last Confederate picket that there were Federals nearby. That's why Father Bixio went into the back of the wagon to change into the Federal uniform. Joe was also supposed to play mute around any Federal soldiers. They came upon a Federal encampment after about an hour.

Father told the regimental adjutant he was a chaplain and he would celebrate Mass for any of the Catholic soldiers, and he would proclaim the word of God to all others who were interested. The adjutant mentioned that he was Catholic as were about one-third of the men.

Before dinner, Father celebrated Mass, with Joe acting as his helper. Joe would do what he had learned as an altar boy several years before. The regimental commander invited Father Bixio and Joe for supper, which was nice because they hadn't eaten much in two days.

At supper, the adjutant asked Father where he was from, and he replied, "In the Old Country, you mean?" Before the adjutant could answer, Father said he was from a town in northern Italy, and he said the name of the village. Not allowing the adjutant time to think, Father continued, "Yes, I miss where I grew up, but young man, it is my charge to help you all get to heaven, so it doesn't really matter about me then, does it?"

You could tell by the look on the adjutant's face that he was reflecting on Father Bixio's words. He asked no further questions, but you could tell he admired the priest. Though neither of them knew it at the time the three would meet again in the future.

It was good to have a full stomach and a cot to sleep on. The Federal forces hadn't suffered the effects of the war like the Confederacy had. Before retiring, Father Bixio visited the adjutant to get some information. He was inquiring about a field hospital of any kind, so that he could visit with any seriously wounded soldiers and offer them the sacrament of the sick.

Joe fell asleep before Father came back, so he didn't find out until morning what the plan was.

Apparently, there was a field hospital near Winchester, which was about another day's ride. Father Bixio changed, from his borrowed Federal uniform, into something less obvious. Joe enjoyed the priest's company, especially at night.

Father Bixio showed Joe some of the Ignatian exercises of which the Jesuits practiced daily. Father suggested that Joe do the examination of conscience every evening. It was difficult at first, but it got easier with time. The transgressions which Joe had committed in the past came to mind.

Joe realized that his greatest transgressions, or sins, were acts of omission as compared to acts of commission. Father Bixio mentioned that those can weigh heavily on the soul, because they are normally glossed over or forgotten. For that reason, Father said it was important to do an examination of conscience every night., so that you knew what you had to work on.

Father showed Joe how to do imaginative prayer one night, based on Saint Ignatius of Loyola's writings. He explained it as a way of entering into the life of Jesus, by using our God-given gift of imagination. When Joe asked for an example from the bible, Father used the Prodigal Son parable in order to show Joe what he meant.

He told Joe to try to put himself into the shoes of everyone in the story. First, he was supposed to imagine he was the wayward son, going through each step of the Gospel story. Then he was supposed to imagine that he was the son who stayed home, and how he would have felt. Lastly, he was supposed to be the father who was overcome with joy.

Father Bixio ended that exercise by repeating word for word from Luke's Gospel, what the father said to the son who stayed home, "My son, you are here with me always; everything I have is yours. But now we must celebrate and rejoice, because your brother was dead and has come to life again; he was lost and has been found."

Father gave Joe some good news about their seventh night out of Staunton. The news was most appropriate in that Father Bixio had shown Joe how to use Saint Ignatius' imaginative prayer exercise the night before, using the parable of the Prodigal Son.

Father Bixio explained how Sam O'Leary approached him with a dilemma, and he asked Father for some guidance. The dilemma was that he was hesitant to let Joe write to his folks, like he had asked. He feared that because their arrangement might come to light, it could somehow be exposed if he let Joe write home. Understanding Sam's dilemma, Father Bixio offered to write a note to Joe's parents, so that Sam no longer had to worry. That was agreeable to Sam, so they had decided not to tell Joe until the time was right. Father decided the seventh night was exactly that right time.

Father Bixio tried to remember what he put in his letter as best he could, but he could only remember one thing for certain. He told Joe's parents he was able to receive the sacraments frequently.

It turned out that the reason Father Bixio had Joe tell him about the way his family celebrated Christmas, in detail, was because he put a snippet of one of those stories into the letter. That way Joe's parents would know the letter was genuine. He was also sure to mention Joe's sister by name, as an added reassurance to his parents that the letter was the truth.

Father Bixio explained to Joe how he sent the letter with a priest, to give it to another priest, until it eventually wound up in Waterbury, Connecticut. "There's no north or south in heaven. Just right and wrong." Father Bixio had said that on more than one occasion, but especially in regard to sending the letter across the lines. Father said he wished he could have done more, but Joe said it was enough that his parents knew he was alive.

On their way back to Staunton, Joe was overjoyed that his parents knew he was safe. And, Father Bixio was delighted that he got the much-needed medical supplies for the hospital in Staunton. The doctors and nurses back in Staunton were grateful for what Father Bixio had done for them.

If there had been any distrust of Joe by the people of Staunton, those feelings were put to rest with the much-needed supplies. They realized Joe Sullivan had taken a big chance by helping them.

Although the trip wasn't as bad as being in a prisoner camp, he was glad to get back with the O'Learys. He could sleep in a real bed and sit by a fire.

The fireplace was particularly welcomed because one of the nights, when the two were up north, the temperature got so cold, that he shivered horribly during the night. Joe wasn't sure how Father Bixio did it because he was a good 25 years older than him. He remembered that Father Bixio even gave him one of his blankets because he was shivering so much.

The large stack of wood that Joe cut prior to his departing was all gone when they returned. He was sorry that Sara Ann had to cut wood in the cold and snow. He made up for it by cutting wood for the next day-and-a-half.

For the other half day, Joe went with Father Bixio to the hospital. Angela hadn't been at the hospital when they dropped off the medical supplies, so Joe was longing to see her. When Joe walked into the hospital, he visited with Angela, and she was as happy to see him as he was to see her. In fact, she said as much. Joe reached into his coat pocket and pulled something out. He handed it to Angela and said, "This is for you."

Angela carefully unwrapped Joe's gift. It was a hand carved nativity scene. She didn't know what to say, but finally she was able to get out, "This is so nice. Where did you get it?"

Joe told Angela that he whittled it for her when he and Father Bixio weren't doing anything on their trip. He said that he hoped she would put it some place, so that it would remind her of him every time she looked at it. She said she would put it on her family's mantle, which they could see clearly from where they ate their meals. She added that she would include a prayer for Joe in their grace before eating.

When Angela asked Joe about the trip, he told Angela he thought the Federal forces were strong, and that they would be to Staunton by the spring.

He also confided in her that he was worried for their safety when the Federals did arrive. His feelings were based on the lessons of history, and he prayed that this would be different. Still, he told Angela to be careful and not to give anyone cause to harm her.

Angela wasn't sure where Joe's new-found information came from, but he told her that the Federals were less than two days of hard riding from Staunton. He didn't think they would do anything till the spring, so that they could build up their strength, but he said you never know. In that some of the wounded soldiers were close and could hear, Joe figured he should stop talking and just enjoy Angela's company.

Sam picked Joe up from the hospital about an hour before sundown. He was a bit somber all the way back to the farm because he worried what would happen to Angela and the O'Learys. He could be repatriated by the spring.

He didn't worry about Father Bixio because the Italian priest had such a pleasing disposition about him. It was hard not to like him. Joe just hoped that none of the Federals, who they encountered on their northern foray, would discover that he was getting supplies for the Confederacy.

It was a hard winter, and the food supplies were sparse in the valley. The valley had been the breadbasket of the Confederacy, and now they were almost as bad off as the rest of the Old Dominion. Joe noticed that Sara Ann served smaller portions, but they were still blessed to get some food.

Grandpa O'Leary would trap at night, and he would bring the results of his hunting trips to his daughter-in-law. Some of his trips were more successful than others, but he had more difficulty as the winter dragged on.

Sam wished that he had been smarter about storing supplies in the root cellar, because they were down to just eating pumpkins and cucumbers by early February. While the war in Virginia was slow during the winter, Sam heard accounts of the western campaign. Things were not going well for the Confederacy, and the Federals had taken Chattanooga the previous November.

Father Bixio paid a visit to the farm, one day in late winter, to talk to Sam and Joe privately. He said he was going to go on another foray to get as many medical supplies as he could. When Joe asked when they were leaving, Father Bixio said he couldn't go this time. He explained that one of the postmaster's friends discovered what they were doing and he told the provost of Harrisonburg.

He explained that it was dangerous enough for him to go, but at least if he got caught, he could explain his way out of it. However, Joe was a Federal soldier. If he opened his mouth his accent would give him away, and he could be put to death.

While Father didn't have to come to tell Joe that, he did need him to do some things while he was away. Father Bixio gave Joe a key to the church, and he asked him to keep a watch on it. Joe felt honored that the priest would have asked him to do that, because there were any number of well-established parishioners who could have done it.

Father Bixio's premonition had been right. He was found out. While the Federals could have hanged him for what he did, namely stealing medical supplies, they just held him in a jail in Winchester for 12 days. They figured the old priest would learn his lesson, and not do it again.

While Father Bixio was away Joe went to the church and cleared away the snow that had piled up at the front door. He also did some minor repairs. One day, while Joe was there, he got a surprise visit. It was from John, Robert and Martin, the three patients he had helped.

They were hoping they would find Father Bixio at the church, but they were delighted that Joe was there instead. They had been released and they wanted to stop by for a visit. Joe invited the three into the room where Father Bixio generally entertained visitors. While the men sat down, Joe lit the stove and put a pot of coffee on. They didn't say they wanted anything to drink, but Joe remembered what the Italian priest said; people are more relaxed over coffee.

While the four sat looking at the coffee pot, Martin spoke. "Well, Joe, we wanted to tell Father Bixio that we were returning to our companies. Unfortunately, we don't know where they are, so we asked the provost what we should do. He will attach us to the forces guarding the rails until he finds out where our units are.

"We all appreciate what you did for us, and now we can get on with our lives. None of us want to have to kill again, and we mentioned that to the provost."

"Couldn't you go home?" Joe asked, "You've certainly done your share."

"No, we must do this," Martin chimed in. "It wouldn't be right for us not to fight when there is nothing physically wrong with us. Besides, we owe it to our friends who died."

All three men were nodding their heads when Martin said that. When the last sips of coffee were gone, the three men shook Joe's hand and asked him to thank Father Bixio for them.

Joe watched as the three men walked down the street towards the train depot. He wondered if any of them would make it home after the war or if they would meet the same fate as their friends who died in battle.

As Joe was locking the church doors he heard, "Hello, Joe!" He turned to see Angela walking up the steps. A sudden rush of blood went to his face, and he could feel the sensation.

"How are you, Angela? You must have just passed Martin, John and Robert. They were here to see Father Bixio, but he's still not back. I hope he is alright."

"Yes, I am also worried about him. This is much longer than his other trips. Let's pray that he is safe, and that he returns soon."

The two stood on the church steps for about 10 minutes talking. Joe offered to reopen the doors so they could seek some warmth in the church. Angela couldn't, however, because she needed to get home to tend to her ill father. She described how her father had gotten progressively worse since his cough started the week prior. She hoped she didn't bring anything bad home from the hospital.

Joe reassured her that her father wasn't sick because of her, but she wasn't so sure. Joe could feel his face return to normal after Angela left. Was he falling in love with her? This was unsettling because he feared that the spring would test people's nerves as the Federal forces closed in on Staunton.

Though Joe wasn't a strategist, he realized that Staunton was a railway crossroads. From there, trains ran west to Clarksburg, south toward Chattanooga, and east toward Richmond, the seat of the

Confederacy. If he knew that, then he was sure the generals in Washington would set their sights on destruction of the rail lines.

The fact that the Shenandoah Valley was the breadbasket of the Confederacy made Staunton a more important target. If the Federals stopped the flow of food, they could slowly starve the Confederacy.

Joe watched Angela until she was out of sight, then he reopened the church door and decided to go and pray by the tabernacle near the altar. One of Joe's jobs was to make sure the tabernacle candle stayed lit, showing the eternal presence of Jesus. He had, in fact, changed the sanctuary candle the day before. As he prayed, he watched the candle flicker through the red glass holder. He prayed for Father Bixio's safe return, followed by Mr. Quinlan who, according to Angela, was very sick. Then Joe prayed that John, Robert, and Martin fared well as they returned to military service. Lastly, he prayed for his mother, father, sister and his brother; Mark was somewhere at sea.

After relocking the church doors Joe returned to the O'Learys. He didn't realize where the time had gone and he felt somewhat guilty that he fell behind on his chores. He would make it up to them somehow, though he didn't know how right then. Before supper, Joe figured out how to redeem himself.

Joe prayed out loud before dinner, and it was a prayer that spoke to everyone's hearts. He prayed first for Thomas O'Leary, and that he would be protected by his guardian angel. Then, he prayed for Father Bixio's safe return, and for Mr. Quinlan who had been ill for well over a week. Lastly, he prayed that the conflict would come to an end, and that the two sides would heal their wounds with God's providential guidance.

As everyone was praying with head bowed, Sam happened to look around the table. He was amazed that his children were so quiet and not restless. Sara Ann had a peaceful look about her, and Joe looked aglow as he offered this great prayer from his heart.

"Thank you, Joe. That brought me such peace," Sara Ann said. "You have a gift with prayer."

That night, when Joe retired, he thought about what Sara Ann said, but he didn't read too much into it. He slept well that night, and he had a dream about his family. The dream was of when Brigid first went off to school. Everyone was so anxious about that event, but Brigid didn't fret. She said in the dream that she was looking forward to the day when she could receive Jesus in Holy Communion. Joe woke up shortly after that.

By mid-March there was a hint of spring, but then that feeling of happiness was wiped away when about a half-a-foot of wet snow blanketed everything. In fact, one of the roofs at the train station collapsed from the weight of the snow.

Father Bixio had been back for a couple days, and he hadn't let his incarceration ruin his spirits. In fact, one of his Federal captors, a Catholic himself, gave the Italian priest a basket of things which he had snuck into the priest's wagon. The Federals repatriated the Federal blue uniform, however, so that Father Bixio wouldn't have it so easy the next time he felt bold.

A few days after his return, Father Bixio asked Joe for an update on things while he was away. Joe told him about his visit from Robert, Martin, and John. Father Bixio smiled, but he didn't let on that he knew that was going to happen. He just wasn't sure of the timing.

What no one knew was that before Father Bixio had left for his perilous journey, he visited the military commander responsible for Staunton. He gave him a heads up that three men might be coming to see him. He explained each soldier's case in detail, as he knew it. When the three men showed up, taking his cue from the priest, the provost attached the three men to the same company guarding the railway station.

If Father Bixio hadn't done that, the three men would have been scattered and maybe have a setback. Unfortunately, while the concept was right, in the months to come, the outcome wasn't as beneficial as Father Bixio had hoped. In late March, Father found out where the men were, and he extended them an invitation to join himself, Miss

Quinlan, and Joe Sullivan for a picnic after church on March 27th, which happened to be Easter Sunday. The provost was also invited, which made it more likely the three would be there.

A few days before Easter, Joe asked Sam if they could speak after supper while Sara Ann was readying the children for bed. According to the Union-leaning paper in town, the Federals were making a big push south. They even quoted Lt. General Grant, who said it was the Union's plan to suffocate Virginia and not allow them to move troops between theaters. The North would apply pressure in all directions, and Staunton was listed as a key to the fall of Richmond.

With that being common knowledge in Staunton, Joe wanted to ask Sam how that would work out for him. Sam wasn't sure what Joe was getting at, but when Joe asked what obligation he had to him and the Confederacy as far as their arrangement went, Sam understood.

He sat back in his rocker and said, "Joe, I would say as soon as the Federals enter Staunton you can consider our arrangement over. I don't look forward to that day, but I'm afraid it will be here soon. I will miss you when you leave. You have been most helpful, and you've been a complete gentleman. Your father and mother raised you well."

Joe didn't say anything else. He just sat there and stared out the front door. The view from where he sat was beautiful. He could see the mountains to the east as their tops caught the setting sun to the west. That night when Joe retired to his bed, he prayed that the town of Staunton would be treated mercifully. While his beginnings in Staunton were a bit strained, he had been accepted, and he got to like the people. As he lay there in bed, he wondered how it would all work out, and what he should do.

Should he just wait until he was repatriated? Or, should he walk into town to Saint Francis and wait with Father Bixio? The latter seemed more likely, so he would be sure to ask Father Bixio if that was alright with him. Joe prayed for the O'Learys, Father Bixio and Angela. He also hoped and prayed that there wouldn't be a big loss of life when that day came.

10

Cause for Joy

Patrick Sullivan rushed home from work because he was so excited about the news he read. The Union was making a strong push towards Richmond. This news meant that Joe would possibly be freed by the summer.

When Patrick got to the house there was a visitor, it was Father Hendricken. Father had decided to stop by on the way to another parishioner's house. Their parish priest was in a good mood, for some reason, and Patrick could tell that Ellie had just told their parish priest something funny. The priest was still snickering as he stood up to shake Patrick's hand.

"Ellie was just sharing a story with me about Mark, and I found it tremendously funny."

Patrick looked at Ellie with an inquisitive look on his face, and she said, "It was the story of when Mark got on the wrong ship somewhere because he had consumed too many spirits."

It was a funny story, but not for their son, as Patrick recalled. Mark couldn't go ashore for three whole months.

Father Hendricken knew about Joe being alive and well, so that was one of the reasons for his visit. He had also seen the write-up in the paper and wondered if they had heard any additional news. Ellie and Patrick related to Father that there had only been one other piece of news out of Staunton, and it was also signed J.B.

That piece of news communicated that Joe was doing as well as could be expected, and he was treated well. Contained within the letter was a piece of news that only Joe could have known. That news was about Father Hendricken and something he did for one of his parishioners, which really gained everyone's admiration, but especially young Joseph Sullivan.

After Father Hendricken left the Sullivans, Ellie and Patrick recounted that life changing event some five summers prior. A fight broke out down the street from Immaculate Conception, and when the priest heard the commotion he went to see what was happening. The priest, who was of slight build, walked right into the middle of the confrontation, and he stood between the two who were throwing punches. One of those involved was a parishioner and the other wasn't.

When the parishioner got knocked to the ground, Father Hendricken approached the one still standing and grabbed him around his chest. The sight of the much smaller priest holding the much larger man was amazing.

The man tried and tried to shake loose whoever was holding him, but he couldn't break free. All the while, Father Hendricken was speaking into the man's left ear, saying, "now, now, that's enough. Let's go down to the church and the three of us can talk this over." When the man realized it was a clergyman who was restraining him, he finally stopped. Though the whole crowd was egging them on, Father Hendricken would only let the two ruffians come with him, and he didn't do that until the crowd dispersed.

Joe didn't witness the incident, but he heard his two older brothers talk about it. Though no one ever heard what caused the brawl, the two ruffians became good friends because of whatever Father Hendricken talked to them about.

11

Day of Reckoning

On the 3rd of June, Sam's father came to the farm and told Sam and Sara Ann that the Federals were near Harrisonburg. Unlike other close calls, he expected the worst for Staunton, since it was a vital rail crossroad.

Sam's father seemed to spend a lot of time in the barn, and Joe found out why when he was bringing a horse in for the night. Mr. O'Leary was putting supplies under the barn, in a hideaway not easily found.

Mr. O'Leary and Sam figured the Federals would take everything that wasn't nailed down, so his dad was squirreling away things in advance of the Federal's arrival. When Mr. O'Leary realized Joe had seen him, he told Sam. Sam didn't feel he had to mention anything about it, because he knew Joe wouldn't tell the Federals about the cache of food and other war contraband.

At breakfast two mornings later, Sam told Joe to get his belongings, so he would take him to Saint Francis'. Sam heard that the Federals had defeated the Confederacy near Piedmont, and they would probably be in Staunton the next day.

Joe was overjoyed that he would be reunited with his family soon, but he still felt sorry for the O'Learys. Sara Ann and the children gave Joe warm hugs and kisses, and there were also some tears. Going outside, Joe stood on the porch and gazed at the view he had grown accustom to over the past ten months. He climbed up in the wagon, and Sam handed Joe the reins. There wasn't much talking on the way to town, but each man knew he was indebted to the other. Besides wearing his uniform, Sam wore his artificial arm because he wanted to show Joe his appreciation.

When they pulled up to the church, Father Bixio happened to be out front. He was gardening. They could hear gunfire in the distance, but it didn't seem to faze the Priest. When he saw Joe, he stopped what he was doing and walked down the steps to the street. He went to Sam's side of the wagon and shook hands with Sam. Father Bixio knew to shake Sam's left hand, but he was caught off guard when he saw an arm resting on Sam's right leg.

Father smiled when he noticed the artificial arm, and said, "I see Joe has been busy whittling." Father Bixio never met Sam before the war, so he was pleasantly surprised with how he would have looked with two arms. Joe, however, had shared with Father about the first time he saw Sam at Gettysburg sitting up in his saddle. Father tried to conjure up that image of Sam, but he was brought back to the moment when he realized the canon fire, and gunshots were getting closer.

"I believe they are getting closer by the sound of the canons," Father said. Sam turned his head slightly towards the sound of the noise and responded, "Yeah, I suppose they will be here sometime tomorrow. Please make sure Joe stays in the church until you talk to someone in authority."

Joe felt a tear drop on his right cheek, and he noticed that Sam also had tears streaming down his cheek. They were both so choked up that the best that either of them could do was nod.

"I will write when I can," Joe said.

Sam just said, "You take care of yourself, and thanks for all you did for me and my family. I will write back."

With that Sam released the brake, picked up the reins with his left hand, and said, "Let's go home before the Federals get here."

12

Freed

For supper that night Father Bixio had somehow procured a chicken, but that wasn't what was great about dinner. To Joe's delight, Angela came by to say hello and goodbye. Though Father didn't say anything about that, Joe knew he had somehow arranged her visit. He left the two alone for what seemed like an hour, while he went to visit a sick parishioner.

When Father came back, Angela stood up and took Joe by the hand. She was going to say something, but she started to cry instead. Joe didn't know what to do, so he took her in his arms and said, "Everything will be alright. I promise I will help you in any way I can."

That wasn't what Angela wanted to hear, but it was good enough.

"Joe, you take care of yourself, and don't forget me."

At that she turned and started to leave, but Joe regained his composure and said, "Angela, I have strong feelings for you. I looked forward to whenever I could see you, and if things were different, I would have liked to stay with you."

Angela rushed back to Joe, hugged him, and kissed him. Then, she was ready to leave. She started crying again as she ran out without looking back.

The next morning it got very noisy right before noon. Joe remembered the time because the church bells chimed twelve times right after the increased noise. Father Bixio went out shortly after he gave Joe his blessing, and he told him he was going to find someone of authority.

About an hour later, Father Bixio came back into the church with a Union soldier. It wasn't just any soldier, it was the adjutant who treated them so nicely on their first trip for supplies.

Father Bixio tried to explain as best he could what had happened to Joe, but the Captain wanted to hear it from Joe's mouth.

"Corporal, I'm glad you can really talk," remembering that he thought Joe was a mute the first time they met. "You can tell me your story," the Captain said.

For the next ten minutes, Joe and the adjutant talked. Initially, the adjutant was irritated that Joe had helped Father Bixio pilfer supplies, but with Joe's descriptions of the conditions they were facing, he understood. The adjutant told Joe that he might face a court martial for treason, but he said that he would personally get statements from Father Bixio, Miss Quinlan, and Captain O'Leary.

The next several days were noisy in and around Staunton. The Federals blew up parts of the rail lines, storage depots, and other things they deemed would hurt the "Secessionists," as many of the Federal soldiers referred to them.

Joe was reattached to a unit, so that he could draw a uniform issue and supplies. When Joe went to the quartermaster's tent, he was amazed at everything they had. Joe asked if he could maybe get some extra hardtack. They obliged, with no questions asked.

What the adjutant said regarding the court martial was true, but no one seemed to be in a rush. Joe could go visit the O'Learys, and he brought them some food, though he didn't tell that to the quartermaster. The quartermaster just assumed Corporal Sullivan was making up for lost time as a prisoner.

As expected, the prisoners at Richmond did not fare as well. Shortages of everything, but especially food, had taken a severe toll on his comrades. He would never forget Sam and Sara Ann's kindness when it came to food. They never held back.

Joe also got to see Father Bixio, and while he tried to see Angela, he was unable. Apparently, a Federal soldier tried to have his way with her, and she successfully fended off the drunken soldier's attack. However, she was too cut-up and disfigured to see Joe. She didn't want him to remember her like that. Plus, she knew he might get mad and do something to jeopardize his newfound freedom.

While Joe visited with Father Bixio, the Italian Priest told him not to talk like they do in Connecticut. He told him to talk slower and try to lose the accent, if at all possible. The Italian Priest said that before Joe went before the tribunal he might want to put a small stone or chewing tobacco in his mouth. That way, the priest said, as he gave Joe a demonstration with a pebble placed in his mouth, he would have to be deliberate about how he spoke.

Joe was baffled by Father's advice. However, Joe found out at the court martial what the priest was getting at. Father had found out that one of the Union generals who had taken Staunton, specifically Jeremiah Sullivan from Indiana, had the same last name as Joe. Father Bixio had planted the thought in some of the Catholic officers' minds that Joe was the general's nephew.

"And it doesn't seem right to court martial the general's nephew, does it? He was a prisoner of war and only helping out as any good Christian would."

Joe got to tell his whole story at the court martial with few questions asked. The officers thought, after all, that they were talking to General Jeremiah Sullivan's nephew.

Before Joe went into the building, which was used for the court martial, he placed a twist of chewing tobacco between his cheek and gum. Though he didn't like the taste, he knew it could mean the difference between freedom and prison. It was worth a try, and it worked as Father Bixio said.

Joe described the events at Gettysburg in detail, and he shared with the officers how sorry he felt for the soldiers returning from battle the day after he was captured. Then, he told them how he was assigned to the ambulance corps, being promised he would be treated well and fed, if there was any food left. Joe shared with the board of officers how he helped Doctor O'Leary, specifically by how he helped save Doctor O'Leary's brother's life, twice.

Next, Joe told about how it was decided he would stay with Captain O'Leary, who was no longer able to fight, in order to get him home safely to Staunton. He also explained how when some Confederate soldiers came to fetch him with the express purpose of sending him to a prisoner camp in Richmond, Captain O'Leary came up with the idea of keeping Joe to help around the farm.

Joe didn't mention, however, that he was probably responsible for helping feed a multitude of Confederate soldiers. He figured that would hurt his cause.

The part that worried Joe the most was his having gone on the forays to help Father Bixio get much needed medical supplies. When Joe explained that he knew he could be hung as a spy if the Confederates found out, it seemed to satisfy everyone.

One of the colonels was interested in Joe's description of how he, Father Bixio, and the nurse had helped the soldiers who weren't of sound mind. It was that piece of information, and the fact that it was believed that he was General Sullivan's nephew, that really helped Corporal Joseph Peter Sullivan.

Joe was found not guilty of treason. In fact, it was felt that he could be of some assistance with the medical corps up north. They had in mind to send Corporal Sullivan to General Hospital # 1 in Frederick, Maryland.

Joe went to see Father Bixio to thank him for all he did for him, and he said he lost his Connecticut accent for the court martial. The two laughed at that, but the final goodbye was not all laughter. There was some disturbing news that Father Bixio shared with Joe.

Father discovered from someone at the military hospital that Robert and Martin had died on the 4th of June. Father didn't know many specifics, but he said it sounded like they did something heroic, so their compatriots could withdraw safely. John, as far as Father Bixio knew, was alright. Joe learned much later that John survived the war and was working for the railroad near Lexington, Virginia.

13

Home

Joe was given a long furlough, so he went home to see his mother, father and Brigid. The decanter was still on the mantle, and though it wasn't Christmas, they pulled the cork. He told them everything that happened to him; from when he was captured at Gettysburg up until his release in Staunton. At places in the description, Joe got emotional and couldn't talk. He would take a nip from his glass, and then he would continue.

When Joe said that Sam reminded him of Paddy, his mother started crying. Joe's father moved next to his wife and gave her a hug to calm her down. Joe continued when his mother stopped crying.

They were curious about who J.B. was and his father said, "What a selfless person he must be."

They were up until the sun went down, and Joe was glad he could sleep in his own bed. He slept so peacefully until the early morning when he was awakened by a loud noise. The noise was from a new factory whistle. His mother said they replaced the former one with a much louder one in the spring.

Since he was up, Joe went to see Father Hendricken, and he stayed for at least two hours. Father wanted to hear everything that happened to Joe, and he left instructions that he wasn't to be interrupted unless someone was dying.

While Joe and Father Hendricken were talking, he remembered that Father Bixio said that Father Hendricken had done a wonderful job teaching the Sullivan family their faith. He also mentioned that the Italian Priest had also said Joe's Latin was better than his altar boys at Saint Francis'.

Joe was going to ask Father Hendricken what it was he did to break-up that fight all those years back, but he decided not to. Some things are better left untold.

Joe's furlough went quickly, and he knew that he had to return to duty. His assignment was to a military hospital near Frederick, Maryland. He would be a hospital steward. At first, they didn't understand how Joe could help them, but then they realized he understood what was locked in the soldiers' minds better than they did.

Joe did his best, but he realized he was missing an important part of the puzzle. In other words, the hospital was missing a priest. Joe tried to remember what Father Bixio said when they were with Robert, Martin, and John, but he had difficulty putting it into words. He wished he had paid better attention to Father Bixio's every word.

While Joe was there he had the opportunity to visit the hospital in Annapolis, Maryland. The U.S. Naval Academy had moved to Providence, Rhode Island the first year of the war in case the Confederacy captured Annapolis. The academy grounds were taken over by the US Army, the original occupant of the property, along the Chesapeake Bay. It was originally called Fort Severn. Besides using the academy for a training area, there was also an Army General Hospital like the one in Frederick.

Joe wrote to Father Bixio, describing what had happened since leaving Staunton. Joe asked that Father deliver the enclosed letters to Sam and to Angela. However, there was no news back, so Joe wondered if the letter even made it to Staunton. It was hard to believe that there was a war going on, since it was very peaceful in Frederick.

Nearly six months passed, and then Joe found out why he never heard back from Father Bixio, Sam and Angela. In September 1864, the Confederacy had retaken much of the Shenandoah Valley, and that was the reason for the upswing in patients at the hospital. His letters never made it to Staunton.

In November, he was asked to drive a group of ladies up to Gettysburg, Pennsylvania. Someone from the hospital had the idea that they should go for the dedication of the cemetery. It turned out that President Abraham Lincoln would perform the dedication. They would have to make the trip in one day, so they left very early.

When they got near Emmitsburg, they could see what looked like a college off to the left. They stopped to get some refreshments and found out that indeed it was a college and a seminary which was called Mount St. Mary's. Two days later, on the way back to Frederick, Joe asked the ladies if they would mind stopping at the college, again.

Joe and the older of the ladies, who was Catholic, walked around the sprawling grounds. The setting was beautiful, because the college seminary sat at the base of a mountain, and thus the name of the school. The school was dedicated to Saint Mary, the Mother of Jesus, so it was fitting to call the school Mount St. Mary's.

Joe and the woman went exploring and they stopped a priest who was outside of what appeared to be the main building. The priest asked if he could help them, and the woman stated they were interested in any history of the college that the priest might be able to offer.

The priest shared the history of the college and seminary as he recalled it, and it had an impressive history. The college was founded in 1808 by a French priest by the name of DuBois. He went on to explain that Father DuBois started the college and that a woman by the name of Elizabeth Anne Seton was encouraged by the priest to start a school for girls across the valley. He explained how Elizabeth Anne Seton founded the Sisters of Charity in America.

Joe, and the ladies enjoyed their visit, and the talk on the way back to Frederick centered on the stop at the college. There was also a brief mention of the goings on in Gettysburg, like whether the Honorable Edward Everett's two-hour speech was overshadowed by the President's brief but skillful address.

In February of the next year, Joe received a promotion. Doctors had complained about working with a corporal, so one of the doctors recommended promoting Joe to Lieutenant. Someone did some checking and discovered there was a precedent. That suited Joe fine because with the promotion came a nicer place to stay. He stayed with an older couple in town, and they liked having someone there who reminded them of their son who was killed at Chancellorsville.

The wounded kept coming into General Hospital # 1 and the hospital had to expand. Joe would visit soldiers, particularly the ones who weren't right in the head. He remembered back to Father Bixio's assessment of lost limbs versus lost minds, and how he thought the latter was worse.

Richmond fell soon after Christmas of 1864, and the remaining Confederate stronghold was Petersburg. Joe asked if he could take a week of leave to go home to Connecticut, but it was denied. They couldn't spare anyone.

However, in the spring Joe asked for a weekend pass, so he could visit Mount St. Mary's. Since stopping the prior November, something was tugging at Joe's heart. He arrived on a Friday night and stayed in a room offered by the same priest who had given them the tour. Joe was able to get a room because attendance had fallen off substantially since those studying for the priesthood were no longer exempt from military service.

Joe spent a lot of time in prayer, talking to the priests, and by the time he went back to Frederick on Sunday afternoon, he knew what he wanted to do for the rest of his life.

Joe felt called to the priesthood. He reflected on his upbringing and remembered Father Hendricken, in particular. Then, he looked fondly on the time he spent in Staunton, Virginia with Father Bixio.

Trying to compare the two priests, Joe saw how they were both committed to helping people.

Both Fathers, Hendricken and Bixio, gave their all to Christ, and they held nothing back. In reading the Bible, Joe saw them particularly in the beatitudes and the scripture verse about when someone asked Jesus, "What must they do?" They both left everything they had and followed Jesus. Joe realized that the two priests did that in more tangible ways than giving away everything. Not only did they give up things in a material sense, but in a spiritual sense as well.

One of the things he learned when he went to Mount St. Mary's was that, to be a priest, you needed a college degree. Then, he learned, the minimum age to be a priest was 24 years-old. Joe prayed on that; and later, he decided he would go to college after the war.

Joe realized one of the reasons he could neither say nor do some of the same things that Father Bixio did, was because he didn't have a grounding in the liberal arts. So, while he was ready to go right to the seminary, he realized college was a necessary requirement.

Directly before Joe's weekend at the Mount, one of the surgeons spoke to Joe about his plans after the war. The doctor was impressed with Joe's medical knowledge and said he would help him to continue to pursue his medical degree, if that's what he wanted.

Joe appreciated the doctor's offer, and he didn't say no right off. While Joe was intrigued by the offer, and admired doctors, he wanted to heal men's souls like both Fathers Hendricken and Bixio. He saw saving souls as more important than saving bodies.

14

War's End

In July 1865, Lieutenant Joseph P. Sullivan was mustered out of the Union Army in Frederick, Maryland. He was anxious to get home as soon as he could to see his parents, sister and brother. Joe hadn't seen Mark since the war started four years prior.

On his arrival in Waterbury he was met by his family, including Mark. Mark had changed a lot in his appearance. Besides a beard, he seemed taller and frailer. As Joe came to find out, his brother had a serious bout of dysentery in the spring, and he lost nearly a third of his body weight.

The mood in Waterbury was like the mood in Frederick, Maryland. People were overjoyed the war was over, and they could resume their lives. Unfortunately, countless sons and husbands wouldn't share in the joyous mood, not to mention the tens of thousands of soldiers, who were missing body parts.

Mass that Sunday was special because the Sullivans all went together. Mark wasn't as fortunate as Joe during the war and to be able to go to Mass proved overwhelming. He was more overjoyed than most, as evidenced by the tears running down his cheeks.

As Father Hendricken processed down the aisle, he stopped at the Sullivan's pew, turned his head and smiled. Joe hadn't had a chance to tell the parish priest his plans yet, because he wanted to tell his parents first. Joe had been home a full day, and the excitement of the war's end was what everyone talked about. Joe would find an appropriate time to tell his parents about his plan.

He still wanted to discern what he was meant to do. Since he had also considered sailing with his brother, he thought he would accompany Mark on a trip to New Haven, which was on the coast.

After a week at home, Joe and Mark went to New Haven. It was good to get to know Mark again. They traveled together for about a week, and in that period of time Joe realized he had more to share with Mark than his brother did with him. Mark's life on board a ship sounded boring to Joe.

The thought of helping Mark with his boating business washed away both literally and figuratively. Joe told his brother about his desire to become a priest, and Mark was supportive of that decision. In fact, he said, "Joe you always seemed to have a way about you. I believe you will be a good priest, and from what you told me about your being knocked to the ground in the heat of battle, it sounds like God has plans for you."

He hadn't told his parents about his desire, but he would tell them when he returned to Waterbury. Mark on the other hand, wasn't going to return to Waterbury, so they said their goodbyes in New Haven.

Mark, as it turns out, would sign onto the crew of a beautiful schooner in New London. It was headed off to some island, or islands in the Caribbean. Though neither of them knew it at that parting, it would be the last time the brothers saw each other.

On returning to Waterbury, the first thing Joe did was to tell his parents about his desire to become a priest. His mother was thrilled, but Joe couldn't tell if his father was as delighted as his mother.

Next, Joe told Father Hendricken about his yearning to become a priest. Joe was surprised at Father Hendricken's response, but when Joe reflected on his response a year later it made sense. Father Hendricken suggested that Joe get a job somewhere and pray on his decision. Father believed that if it was meant to be, it would be. Father Hendricken explained that he knew young men, back in Ireland, who rushed into their decision and then later found that the life of a priest was not their calling.

Joe followed Father's suggestion, and he spent more time in discernment.

15

Time of Discernment

Joe returned to Philadelphia and stayed with his aunt, uncle and two cousins. His Uncle Wilhelm had added on to their house in Philadelphia, so Joe wasn't a bother. His cousins loved hearing about Joe's time as a soldier, particularly the "shooting stuff." His aunt and uncle, on the other hand, loved hearing about Joe's compassionate captors. It was Aunt Kathleen who said, "Joe, you have been so blessed by God and the people he put in your life."

When Joe mentioned that he made Sam O'Leary an artificial arm, his uncle was intrigued. One day at dinner his uncle said there was a company nearby that made artificial limbs, and that he had talked to the owner about Joe. While Uncle Wilhelm enjoyed having Joe work for him, he realized it was probably God's will that Joe should work at the artificial limb company. When he mentioned that to Joe, his aunt said, "Oh, what a splendid idea, Wilhelm. Joe can help the lame walk!"

Joe thought about it, and it did sound like a good idea, so he worked at the artificial limb company for the next several months. He divided his time between making artificial limbs, particularly arms, and helping his uncle make furniture. All the while, he prayed to God, so that he would know what he should do.

During this time of discernment, his aunt was a considerable influence. Though she just casually mentioned it, Aunt Kathleen became involved in a prayer group. Perhaps she joined because of the war. She seemed more holy, if that was possible, and when she talked about God, she seemed to be aglow.

Joe went with his aunt to a parish mission at a Catholic Church about three miles away from their house. Initially, Joe had offered to watch the boys since the visiting priest was from where Wilhelm grew up. However, Wilhelm declined his nephews offer, thinking it was more important for Joe to go, since he had shared with them his desire to be a priest.

The visiting priest who was giving the parish mission was a Redemptorist. He was of the same order as Bishop John Neumann, who had died before the war. Joe could tell his aunt really admired Bishop Neumann, and she may have even talked about him while he stayed with them before the war. Perhaps some of those stories were in his subconscious; he just couldn't recall any.

When Father Francis Xavier Seelos came out to speak, Joe was immediately captivated by the meek looking priest. His message that night was on personal holiness. A very simple statement which Father Seelos made stayed with Joe during the months and years to come. Father Seelos said, "If you want to be happy, be holy. And if you want to be very happy, be very holy."

Perhaps that simple statement was the key to life. Both Fathers, Hendricken and Bixio were very happy people, and Joe believed it was due to their holiness.

After the mission, Joe asked Aunt Kathleen if she wanted to try to see the priest. She was delighted that Joe suggested they go together. The two waited about thirty minutes while the other well-wishers greeted the humble Bavarian priest. The wait was worth it.

When Joe and his aunt greeted the priest, Aunt Kathleen was dumbstruck, and couldn't speak. Joe told Father Seelos how much he enjoyed the mission and shared with him that he believed he was called to the priesthood. Joe told Father Seelos that he was spending a year praying on it, at the recommendation of his parish priest.

Father Seelos replied, "Praying is good, but you shouldn't fixate on time. You will know, Joe, if that's what God is calling you to do. I will keep you in my prayers."

Aunt Kathleen felt embarrassed that she couldn't speak, but she was glad her nephew had a conversation with Father Seelos. When they got home that night, his aunt told Wilhelm about the marvelous experience. Joe went to bed that night and prayed fervently for a sign.

16

The Trumpet Sound

Joe's sign didn't come that night, but it did come two months later. The sign wasn't a trumpet sound and no walls came tumbling down, but Joe knew one day at Mass that he was being called. When the priest elevated the Host during the consecration, Joe heard a whispering sound, which said, "It is time my son. The harvest is plenty, the laborers are few. Come now, be not afraid." Joe turned to see if the person behind him was talking to him, but there was a pewful of children seated behind him. He was quite sure Jesus was speaking to him, but he wanted to be sure.

Ever since he left Staunton, Joe had grown accustomed to practicing the Ignatian exercises that Father Bixio taught him. That is, he placed himself in the context of the gospels. The night before Joe was called, he used the one from Saint John's Gospel about the blind man, and the reading spoke to his heart. Joe read the Gospel passage several times very slowly, shutting his eyes at various points of the story.

He could visualize Jesus stooping towards the ground and spitting into the dirt. Jesus stirred the spittle around and worked it with his fingers making a clay-like substance. He did this while he was still talking with his disciples, saying that neither the man's parents nor the blind man sinned. Jesus said it was so the works of God might be made visible through him.

Standing up, Jesus rubbed the moistened earth over the blind man's eyelids, as if He were anointing him with holy oil. The man just stood there letting Jesus do as He wished. It was almost as if the blind man could feel power coming out from the man they called Jesus.

Then, Jesus told the man to go wash in the Pool of Siloam. That seemed odd at first to Joe, but he figured one of Jesus' disciples would have taken him there. He imagined that one of Jesus' disciples, maybe even the Apostle John, volunteered to take the blind man to the Pool of Siloam and told him that he should do as Jesus instructed. He visualized the disciple telling the blind man that if it was God's will, then he would have his sight.

Joe wondered how a man who was born blind could know what he was looking at when he regained his vision? Joe reflected on that specific part of the Gospel passage, and he had an epiphany.

While the disciple was taking the blind man to the Pool of Siloam, the blind man would have had certain visions. Maybe even visions of a man condemned to die several days later, walking the same path he was now taking, but out of the city. The blind man could see in his mind the scourging, the crowning with thorns, and then the carrying of the cross to Golgotha. He would learn from that walk what Jesus looked like and remember the lines read to him from Isaiah, "By his stripes we were healed."

Joe imagined that the blind man even questioned whether he wanted to be able to see if the world was as cruel as he saw in his visions. However, to dismiss that question in his mind the blind man saw a woman, who he was told was Jesus' mother weeping, and yet another woman wipe his face with a cloth when Jesus fell to the ground under the weight of the cross. The blind man, when he saw the love of those two women, and then a third at the foot of the cross, resolved to love as they loved.

It all made sense to Joe in the context of that passage from John's Gospel, that Jesus came to give sight to the blind. The disciple helped the man step down into the Pool of Siloam and he watched as the blind man washed his face. After the man was sure he got all the dirt off his face, he looked towards the sky. He saw the azure sky and some wispy clouds. Then, the man proclaimed, "I can see, I can see." The disciple who helped him said, "Praised be God."

Joe also remembered Father Bixio stating that in John's Gospel, in the very last line it said, "There are also many other things that Jesus did, but if these were to be described individually, I do not think the entire world would contain the books that would be written." Joe found that by doing the divine reading, in the context of what was written before and after the passage, it made the Gospel stories of Jesus come to life.

In December, Joe received a three-page letter from Father Bixio. In that letter, besides giving updates on most everything that had happened since the end of the war, he told Joe how much he missed his company. He shared that when Joe left, he felt sadness because he was unable to hear Joe's stories about growing up. He told Joe that his stories reminded him a lot of his own childhood in the town of Bolsano, Italy. Like Joe, he said he had a loving mother, father and several brothers and sisters.

Joe wrote Father Bixio in return, and he shared with him his desire to become a priest. Before mailing it, Joe meditated on it and tried one of the spiritual exercises that Father Bixio had shown him.

About a week after Joe mailed the letter to Father Bixio, he received a letter from Sam O'Leary. It was a long letter and he shared many of the things that happened in the year-and-a-half since Joe was liberated.

Sara Ann and he welcomed another child during the summer, so they were now a family of five. His brother Tom returned and works at a hospital but was planning to start a private practice when he was able. Two pieces of news really took Joe by surprise.

The first was that Father Bixio had to leave Saint Francis Church. Though Sam didn't know the exact details, he felt it had to do with his forays behind "enemy lines." When Joe read that line, he stopped and smiled. He closed his eyes and thought about the first foray he and Father Bixio went on together, and he remembered one of Father Bixio's statements to the Federal adjutant. "It is my charge to help you all get to heaven."

Glancing back down at the letter, he continued reading. Sam believed Father Bixio was going to California, but he wasn't certain. He said that Father Bixio had asked him to send his best wishes and his regrets that he hadn't answered Joe's letter.

The other piece of news that caused Joe to smile was that Tom had proposed to Angela Quinlan, but she turned him down. She was going to become a nun with the Sisters of Charity.

Sam said Angela left for Richmond in September to work in a hospital there. He wasn't sure of the terminology, but he used the word novitiate in trying to explain her position. That was all he knew, but he said he would visit her dad and try to find out more.

Poor Tom, Joe thought. They would have been good together. He was happy for Angela, though. It appeared that she also had a call to religious life.

Joe knew how invaluable Catholic nuns were during the war. It reminded him of something Father Bixio told a Federal officer on their first foray. "Heaven knows no north or south, I'm just concerned for men's souls."

Several religious orders did much for both sides during the war, but it was probably the Sisters of Charity who did the lion's share of the healing. He remembered watching Angela with the soldiers and how, just by her presence in a room, there was peace. He could only imagine how much good she will do as a nun.

While Joe was visiting a seminary near Philadelphia one weekend one of the priests asked Joe if he felt, "called." Joe didn't answer right away, but he looked the priest in the eyes, and said, "Yes, Father, I do."

Joe explained to the priest what his parish priest had told him about waiting and praying for a year. The priest said that was good advice, since being a priest has demands that will wear out the strongest of men. Since that priest's advice was very similar to Father Hendricken's advice, Joe waited longer.

Joe started college at Mount St. Mary's in the spring. He worked especially hard in his studies and spent his free time helping at Saint Joseph's Parish in Emmitsburg. The elderly priest greatly appreciated Joe's help. Joe was particularly good working with the young kids who were preparing to receive one of their sacraments.

Joe was so busy, he neglected to continue his journaling. For the little bit of journaling that Joe did for those next three years, it was primarily about reflections of his time in Staunton up to entering Mount St. Mary's. Father Michael encouraged Joe to write everything down that he could remember up until the time of his ordination.

Thanks to Father Michael, Joe's journal eventually ended up in the college archives. Fortunately, it was rediscovered by an undergraduate student in 1975, while he was researching a history assignment in the college archives on the "Just War Theory."

17

No Greater Love

With his college degree complete, Joseph Sullivan was accepted into Mount St. Mary's Seminary the fall of 1868. He progressed steadily through his seminary courses. The reason he did so well was that his Latin was far ahead of everyone else's. When asked about that fact, Joe said it was primarily because his parish priest had done such an excellent job. Additionally, he recalled that Father Bixio had helped him when he was in Staunton.

After he was ordained in 1871, Joe volunteered for the Indian missions. He had been fascinated with stories of a Belgian priest who started many mission schools and saved a lot of souls. Joe realized he was fortunate to have been saved from dying at Gettysburg, so he wanted to save other men's souls, if it was the will of God.

In early July 1871, Father Sullivan set off for Minnesota with two nuns to start a school for Indian children to the southwest of Minneapolis, near Fort Ridgely. The journey was difficult, but he was much better off than the other missionaries who preceded him.

He remembered hearing about Father Peter De Smet's travels from Saint Louis, and the hardships he endured to save souls, were legendary. In fact, in comparison to Father De Smet's first travels to the upper mid-west by canoe and horseback, Father Sullivan traveled on steam ship up the Mississippi from Saint Louis.

It had been a dry spring and summer, but for some reason mother nature caught up for lost time. It rained steadily for 10 days, and the river became deadly. In addition to the raging river, other problems overwhelmed the steam paddle wheeler, all at once. First, it was struck by debris, and then the crippled boat took on water. And, as if that wasn't enough, the boiler exploded and the interior of the crippled boat was on fire. While the boat was dead in the water, it was buffeted by extraordinarily heavy winds.

No matter how much the crew tried to keep the boat from swamping, it was no use. The boat sunk, but despite the elements, few died. It certainly could have been worse, had it not been for a few brave crew and one passenger.

The account of what Father Sullivan did, after the boat was engulfed by both water and flames, are recounted from the two nuns traveling with the young priest.

Neither Sister Louise nor Sister Devon were strong swimmers, and as soon as they entered the water they were pulled under by their long black habits. No amount of struggling seemed to help the drowning nuns. However, they both felt someone grab under their arms and pull them up to the surface. Even though the rain and winds were still strong, at least they could gasp for breath once they got to the surface.

The two nuns couldn't see anything in the dark of night, and to make matters worse, the rain pummeled their faces. It wasn't until they reached the rivers bank that they could tell it was Father Sullivan who saved them. After making sure the two nuns were safe, he swam back to where the boat was, so he could help others. He made two such trips, bringing first a mother and her baby and then a large black man. That was the last they saw of Father Sullivan, and as the minutes turned to hours, they feared the worst.

The rain stopped the next day and one of the sailors swam back out to the boat, which was barely visible in the murky water. Though the sailor searched, he could find no living soul. He did, however, pull two bodies from the top deck. The nuns encouraged him to go search again, but he was too scared to go below the top deck for fear of drowning.

After two more days on the shore of the river, the nuns continued their journey to their mission just north of Fort Ridgely, Minnesota. It took them three weeks to get to their destination. As they traveled, they prayed continuously for everyone who was lost on the ship, but most especially for Father Sullivan, who had saved them from certain death.

As if there were a cycle, the next summer was a particularly dry one. The steamboat that had been carrying Father Sullivan was salvaged. In going through the compartments on the bottom deck, they found two bodies. First, there was a body buried by a fallen timber. The part of the body which was exposed to the water was nearly gone due to the ravages of time and hungry fish.

The other body they found had one arm underneath the wooden timber, as if he were trying to move the wood beam off the first body. In the man's other hand was a wooden box. He was dressed in black clothes.

Unlike the other body they discovered, which was grotesque from a year under water, the other body didn't look bad at all. In fact, it was almost as if he had been dead only a brief time.

After they wrestled the wooden box from the dead man's grip, they discovered that the dead man was a priest. When they pried the priest's fingers from the wooden box, they noticed something unusual about his chest area. Coming from the priest's breast pocket area was a glow, almost as if he had a tiny lighted lantern in his pocket.

Setting the wooden box aside, they looked in his pocket and found a small round metal case. There was light emanating from the case, and that is what gave off the glow. Curious, one of the men looked to see what was inside the metal case. Upon opening it, they saw a wafer like substance. When the Catholic man in the group saw the wafer, he blessed himself and said, 'My Lord and my God." He knew what it was, but he didn't know how to explain it to the others. The wafer was a consecrated Host used at communion.

As they watched the Host, it grew brighter and the light was so blinding they all had to shut their eyes. When they could no longer sense any light through their closed eyelids, they opened their eyes.

The Host which had nearly blinded them had disappeared. Amazed by the miraculous disappearance of the Host, one of the men said they should look in the wooden box to see what was in it. The Catholic gentleman agreed to be the one to open it, which he did. When he cleaned the muck and mire off the box, there was a small brass name plate. It was inscribed: "Father Joseph Sullivan."

On closer examination of the box, they were amazed that there wasn't any water inside. There was just a chalice and three small glass bottles. Two of the glass bottles were empty and the third one contained a yellowish liquid, which was holy oil. When the Catholic man removed the lid from the oil, they could all smell a wonderful odor.

The traveling kit, as they would learn later, was an ordination gift from Father Sullivan's parents. The Catholic gentleman, again knew what the contents of the box were and brought it to the closest Catholic Church, which was on the Wisconsin side of the river. The man told everything he saw to the priest.

After the man described everything to the priest, the priest asked him if he could write it all down. The man could neither read nor write, so the man retold the priest everything he witnessed again, and the priest wrote it all down.

They buried the bodies of everyone recovered from the boat, but the priest was the only one given a grave marker, since they could tell who he was from the brass plate.

The penknife in the priest's pocket also made its way to the nearest Catholic Church with the traveling kit and pyx. The person who discovered it was convinced that if he stole it, he would be damned. After all, it had belonged to a priest.

The two nuns, whose lives Father saved, were notified that Father Sullivan's body was recovered. The nuns asked permission to have the body re-interred at the Indian mission, since that was Father Sullivan's earthly destination. It took some doing, but eventually Father Sullivan's body made it to its final resting place near the mission he tried to start.

The nuns made sure the mission bore much good fruit in thanks to God and His instrument, Father Sullivan. The nuns also managed to get the chalice and brass plate. The brass plate was put on Father Sullivan's grave, and the penknife was sent back to the young priest's parents in Connecticut.

The chalice and three bottles stayed with the nuns at the Indian mission. Later the nuns received permission, from their bishop, to use the holy oil to bless the mission every September 8th, which was the anniversary of Father Sullivan's death and the Feast of the Nativity of the Blessed Virgin Mary.

18
Postscript

✂ Father William Corby, the Chaplain for the Irish Brigade, served his flock faithfully until the end of the war. After the war, he had several assignments as a Holy Cross priest. He was President of Notre Dame College from 1866-1872 and again from 1877-1881. Some people believe that the term "Fighting Irish" may be due to Father Corby's association with the Irish Brigade.

There are two bronze statues of Father Corby giving the "Final Absolution" at the Wheatfield where the Irish Brigade engaged the Confederate soldiers on July 2, 1863. The two statues are identical, with one located near the approximate location of his giving the Final Absolution on a large boulder on the Gettysburg battlefield. The second statue is located on the University of Notre Dame campus in South Bend, Indiana. It is displayed in front of Corby Hall.

✂ The Confederate soldier who was wearing the Miraculous Medal was from Savannah, Georgia. His name was Pierre, but he was called Pete. He was originally from Paris, France, and he came to the United States in 1848 when he was four-years-old. The Miraculous Medal he wore around his neck was given to him when he was Confirmed.

Pete grew up hearing the stories of Catherine Labouré and how she had three apparitions of the Blessed Virgin Mary. Catherine was a Daughter of Charity, the order of nuns founded by Saint Vincent DePaul and Saint Louise de Marillac. It was during Catherine's second apparition that the Blessed Mother spoke the following, "Have a medal struck as I have shown you. All who wear it will receive great graces."

After the first two thousand medals were cast, the devotion spread like a wildfire. There were numerous miracles associated with wearing the Miraculous Medal, and thus the name. The location of Pete's Miraculous Medal that Joe Sullivan placed around the Confederate corporal's neck, when he helped bury him, is somewhere between the Potomac River and Winchester, Virginia.

> ✠ Roughly twelve miles south of Gettysburg, in Emmitsburg, Maryland, is the National Shrine of Elizabeth Anne Seton, founder of the American Sisters of Charity. The Sisters of Charity are an offshoot of the Daughters of Charity mentioned above. She is the first native born American Saint, and if you go into the Basilica you will see many beautiful mosaics. There is a mosaic of Saint Catherine Labouré sitting at the feet of the Blessed Mother, plus there are mosaics of the Miraculous Medal, Saint Vincent DePaul and Saint Louise de Marillac.

✠ It was mentioned early on that Caleb Applegate and Joseph Sullivan would meet again. They did in the summer of 1868, before Joe entered the seminary. Joe stayed with the Applegates when he was on his way to visit Staunton.

Caleb went on to become a very successful Episcopalian minister in Winchester, Virginia. During Joe's visit, Caleb talked about the night Captain O'Leary, Joe and himself ate dinner together. The dinner consisted of three fish, and it was the last night before they got to Staunton. Caleb remembered catching the fish, and when they were cooking them, how Captain O'Leary and Joe talked about Jesus after His resurrection from the dead. He remembered that specifically because he felt that was when he was called to ministry.

Caleb became well known for his sermons, and he filled the church pews every Sunday. He also became involved in erecting a war memorial in downtown Winchester to remember the sacrifices of his brothers, Joshua and Isaac, and countless other sons of Winchester.

He and his wife had seven children, which delighted Caleb's parents.

⊙ Sam and Sara Ann O'Leary had one more child after the war, and they named him Joseph. Sam got a job with one of the biggest artificial limb makers in the country. When the company moved from Staunton to Washington, D.C., so did Sam and his family.

Sam and Sara Ann came to Joe's ordination, and attended his first Mass. They were both able to receive Holy Communion at that happy occasion because they both converted to Catholicism a year prior. Sam told Joe that it was because of both he and Father Bixio that Sara Ann and he became Catholic.

Even though Sam wore a more functional artificial arm from the company he worked for, he hung the arm Joe made him over the main door in their house. He put it there to remind him of how cruel war is, but also as a reminder of how your enemy could be your best friend.

Sam took Joe's death especially hard, but he found comfort in his memories of Joe and one conversation in particular. It was the evening Joe shared the story about how he was struck down at the Wheatfield, and he couldn't really explain it.

He remembered asking Joe, if he thought God saved him from death, and Joe just looked at him and smiled. Sam reflected often on how God had other plans for Joe that hot July day on the battlefield. Joe, after all, saved Sam's life twice, and the two nuns from the riverboat to name just three. However, only God would know how many souls Joe saved during his short time on earth.

○ Thomas O'Leary did return to Staunton, but he never started his own practice. Instead, he ran the former Confederate general hospital. While he didn't marry Angela Quinlan, he did marry the woman who nursed him back to health after the war.

Thomas had been seriously wounded during the siege of Petersburg, and the former Emily Ent, a nurse, cared for him. They married two years after the war and they had five children.

○ Patrick McGivney, who was Patrick Sullivan's boss, died in June 1873. His oldest son, Michael, became a Catholic priest. The McGivneys and the Sullivans belonged to the same parish in Waterbury, so the boys all would have had their religious instruction from Father Hendricken. Father Michael McGivney went on to found the Knights of Columbus, the largest Catholic fraternal organization in the world.

○ Angela Quinlan became a Sister of Charity, the order founded by Saint Elizabeth Anne Seton. Initially, she worked in the hospitals in Richmond and Staunton, but then was transferred years later to Saint Agnes Hospital in Baltimore, Maryland. She would often think of Joe and Father Bixio, reflecting on how they healed those three soldiers with love and prayers.

She and Joe never saw each other again after his summer visit in 1868, but she still had the Nativity scene, which he gave her. She usually kept it on the dresser in her room, right next to her Bible, crucifix and rosary.

○ Patrick and Ellie Sullivan attended their son's ordination, and they were delighted to meet the O'Learys. They thanked them both for sheltering Joe during his captivity. Patrick retired from the brass factory in 1881, when his injured leg just gave out. He always said how blessed he was to be able to work for 21 years after the accident.

Ellie taught at the Immaculate Conception school until 1884. She became active in the women's guild and was especially an inspiration for new mothers. She thought about her two departed sons, but not so much in the past tense, but in the future tense. She was convinced that her sons were in heaven, and that she would get to see them someday.

Brigid Sullivan married and had four children; two boys and two girls. She named one of her son's Joseph Peter, and the other Patrick Michael, after her two brothers.

She and her husband belonged to Saint Mary's parish in New Haven, Connecticut. She was happy that they had a young priest from Waterbury, and the Nagatauck Valley, by the name of Father Michael McGivney.

Brigid remembered that her father worked for Father McGivney's father at the brass factory, and that he was quite fond of him. She also remembered that her mother often talked about Father McGivney's mother, whose name was Mary. Her mom always said, "Ah dat Mary McGivney tis a livin' saint if I've ever met one."

Brigid's husband joined the Knights of Columbus and worked closely with Father McGivney until the parish priest was reassigned to another parish.

Mark Sullivan made his dreams a reality. He saved his money for years and then invested it wisely. He was so wise in his investments that he bought a fleet of schooners. He moved to New London, and he lived in a mansion overlooking the Thames River. He thought that was fitting, especially since Joe told him the story about the Thames in London, England.

He was saddened that he couldn't get to his brother's ordination. He was at sea, and even though he prayed fervently for some favorable winds, it didn't come until it was too late to bring him back to the United States. Instead, he would have to remember his brother from the last time they saw each other in New Haven, Connecticut. It was a happy parting as he remembered it.

Mark discovered years after the war, that it was the Sisters of Charity who were responsible for saving his life in New Orleans. With that new-found knowledge, he made it a point to visit Saint Agnes Hospital in Baltimore every year. He primarily visited with Sister Catherine, the former Angela Quinlan. He loved hearing stories about Joe in Staunton, Virginia, or the time which he referred to as Joe's "Southern Absolution." He particularly loved the stories about how Father Bixio and his brother went on "forays," as the Italian priest called them.

Curious as to what happened to Father Bixio who was so instrumental in Joe's Southern Absolution, Mark tracked him down. The simple parish priest from Staunton, Virginia, was hastily reassigned to the San Francisco Bay area in 1866, after it came to light how he helped the Confederacy during the war.

Father Bixio went to a Jesuit college in Santa Clara, just south of San Francisco. Mark corresponded several times by letter, and then he got to visit Santa Clara while on two of his visits to San Francisco.

He was so glad he got to meet Father Bixio, and the two met two times. Both times they met, Mark would share some aspect out of his childhood growing up in Waterbury, Connecticut. As Mark told the stories, Father Bixio sat with his eyes closed and with a smile on his face as he tried to imagine Joe in the story.

Even though Mark didn't have much free time, he took to whittling like his younger brother. He whittled with the same knife the two nuns, whose lives Joe saved, somehow returned to his parents. The first thing he whittled, which took him a year, was a priest standing at the altar with the Eucharist held high over his head.

After hearing the account of the men finding Joe's body and the light emanating from his chest, he went to church as often as he could, so he could receive the Body of Christ. In receiving the Host, Mark felt a close presence to Jesus, and his two brothers.

Made in United States
Orlando, FL
26 May 2024